Jacob's Voices

JACOB'S VOICES

Reflections of a Wandering American Jew

Jerold S. Auerbach

SOUTHERN ILLINOIS UNIVERSITY PRESS
Carbondale and Edwardsville

Copyright © 1996 by Jerold S. Auerbach
All rights reserved
Printed in the United States of America
99 98 97 96 4 3 2 1

Frontispiece: Yakov Shmuel Auerbach

Library of Congress Cataloging-in-Publication Data
Auerbach, Jerold S.
    Jacob's voices : reflections of a wandering American Jew / Jerold
S. Auerbach.
        p. cm.
    1. Auerbach, Jerold S. 2. Jews—United States—Biography.
3. Jews—Cultural assimilation—United States. 4. Jews—United
States—Attitudes toward Israel. I. Title.
E184.J5A937 1996
973'.04924'0092—dc20
[B]   95-39568
ISBN 0-8093-2055-X   CIP

The paper used in this publication meets the minimum requirements
of American National Standard for Information Sciences—Permanence
of Paper for Printed Library Materials, ANSI Z39.48-1984. ⊛

For my grandfather

YAKOV SHMUEL AUERBACH

I will . . . feed you with the heritage
of Jacob your father.
Isaiah 58:14
and
my father

MORRY M. AUERBACH

Remove not the ancient landmark,
which your fathers have set.
Proverbs 22:28

in loving memory

CONTENTS

PREFACE   A CHILD OF THE 1930s, I CONFRONTED HISTORY AT
—————————   an early age. Franklin D. Roosevelt was my
president. He was Good. Hitler was Evil. On December 7, 1941,
when I was five, World War II became my war. "Whistle while you
work," I gleefully recited with friends, "Mussolini is a meanie,
Hitler is a jerk." But air-raid drills in school and nighttime black-
outs frightened me. A month after we visited my cousin Billy, a
young marine home on furlough, he was killed on Tarawa. When
Roosevelt died, everyone I knew cried. Then atomic bombs fell on
Japan. We lit an enormous bonfire at camp to celebrate victory and
peace.

My boyhood world was a menacing place. Nazis. The fifth-grade
bully. Christian crosses, adorning necklaces and churches. But my
family was conspicuously typical. All my grandparents were immigrants from Eastern Europe. My parents were their first-born
American children. And I was the designated repository of all their
fears and hopes about being a Jew in the United States.

To have been the child of Eastern European immigrants, Del-
more Schwartz wrote, was "a special kind of experience." It generated unrelenting tension between past and present, between
Europe and the United States, between Judaism and Americanism.
The self-consciousness of American Jews was so decisively molded
by the legacy of Eastern European immigration that it is all but
impossible to imagine American Jewish history without it. I grew
up in the flickering shadows of these cross-cultural, intergenerational encounters.

I was the child of children of those immigrants. The cautious pirouette my parents danced around issues of American Jewish identity seemed perfectly normal to me. I intuited their revision of the classic formula of Jewish emancipation: they were, like everyone else we knew, marginal Jews at home and wary Americans on the street. While my parents performed their cultural highwire act, precariously in transition from Judaism to Americanism, I located my own secure refuge, remote from Jewish memory and at the edge of American Jewish amnesia.

But my childhood unfolded on the historical fault line of Jewish terror and wonder. My ninth birthday coincided with the liberation of Auschwitz; within a week of my twelfth birthday, a Jewish state was born. I belonged to the last generation of Jews to know the horrific consequences of Jewish powerlessness and the first to experience the astonishing restoration of Jewish national sovereignty. I might have been too preoccupied with baseball to notice much else; nonetheless, my interior consciousness was indelibly imprinted by the fate of Eastern European Jewry, by the Holocaust and Israel.

My generation came of age between wartime heroes and student rebels. Too young for the military glory of World War II, we would be too old (or, at least, too inhibited) to gyrate to the antiwar protests of the sixties. Even in New York, we grew up slowly, apprehensively. In our teens, we became the Silent Generation. Occasionally, I felt cheated by my fortuitous escape from the crises that came either too soon or too late to engage me in their public drama. But I enjoyed the private space that accompanied these whims of generational timing.

The tenacious grip of the past, Irving Howe observed, once sustained "a mysterious sense" of Jewish distinctiveness. But the wrenching encounters of Eastern European immigrants, first with the American *goldene medina* and then with their own children, have subsided. For so long the staple of much that was distinctive in American Jewish life and literature, they have by now receded into dim memory. The Lower East Side belongs to someone else. The Holocaust is mendaciously universalized into a multicultural extermination. Intermarriage is the Jewish norm rather than the exception. The very notion of Jewish distinctiveness is suspect. Jews, after all, are at home in America.

If the Jewish past no longer inspires Jewish creativity, what does? American possibilities certainly have enlarged and emboldened the Jewish literary imagination. Writers have been liberated, finally, from the theme of Eastern European immigrants and their American progeny. Just a few years ago, in *Writing Our Way Home*, Ted Solotaroff and Nessa Rapoport confidently proclaimed the arrival in the United States of a new generation of "Jewishly educated and culturally confident" writers, formed by "an unprecedented degree of Jewish diversity, self-expression, security, and influence." Here, now, everything "from neo-Orthodox yuppies to New Age kabbalists" can flourish. As Ms. Rapoport exults, "Having won our place in American culture, we are beginning to be confident enough to reclaim Jewish culture."

Perhaps. But I suspect that American freedom encourages varieties of pro-choice Judaism that are merely an ephemeral fashion show within the larger sweep of Jewish history. Once I believed otherwise. I, too, imagined that the American future, vastly more inspiring than the Jewish past, would mercifully obliterate it. My generation, after all, eluded the Old World constraints of our grandparents and the American inhibitions of our parents. To us, everything was possible.

We proudly migrated from wholesale and retail to the professions. Our striking display of social mobility completed a three-generational journey from rags to riches (or, at least, to judicial robes and academic gowns) that is without American historical parallel. The legal and scholarly professions became our metaphorical cities of refuge. They symbolized our Jewish yearning, while we were still marginal Americans, to identify with the dominant values of our American national home. Once Jews were authorized to interpret the Constitution, to write American history, to explicate the meaning of American literary texts, to analyze American social institutions—that is, to explain the United States to other Americans—our successful absorption was completed.

If acculturation issues were the cards that fate dealt my generation of American Jews, then it must be said that we played them with consummate skill. Without inherited names, wealth, or any status other than what we earned for ourselves, we converted private expectations and public opportunities into a winning hand.

Now that more of our careers lie behind than before us, however, it may be time to reflect on the meaning of the game we played. I wonder whether we fulfilled our American opportunities at the expense of our Jewish responsibilities. Most of all, I wonder what our children can possibly learn about themselves as Jews if we do not remember what we are instructed to teach them.

Most of my contemporaries, by now, seem comfortable as Americans of the Jewish persuasion. Yet the perennial challenge remains: how to be both American and Jewish. I emphasize "both" to distance myself from the legions of American Jews who still insist that Americanism and Judaism form a seamless web. For some, the imagined fusion is a passion for social justice (Jewish source: the Hebrew Prophets). For others, it is a commitment to freedom under the rule of law (Jewish source: the Torah). Or even a fondness for critical intellectual inquiry (Jewish source: rabbinical exegesis).

This fallacy of congruity still contributes to the persistent sublimation of Jewish interests in universal causes (Jewish source: Marx and his modern progeny of non-Jewish Jews). It represents an enduring, remarkably successful acculturation strategy. It was devised to reassure American Jews that they were still Jewish even after they had become American and, perhaps, to reassure the Christian majority that Jews were genuinely American even though their cultural contortions indicated that they still were most assuredly Jewish.

Unlike so many American Jews of my generation, I remain stubbornly inclined to assert the claims of Jewish memory. Here is what I remember.

Jacob's Voices

JACOB, MY GRANDFATHER, CAME TO VISIT WHEN I WAS FOUR years old. I still remember his austere gentleness. He sat, silent and erect, in the sunlit front room of our modest apartment in a two-family house in Forest Hills. Although his words and gestures quickly evaporated, my vivid memory of Jacob endured. Occasionally, I reminded my father of his father's visit—an implicit plea, surely, for Jacob to return. But Jacob never came again.

Whenever I asked about Jacob, my father seemed bemused. Each time, with a touch of impatience, he would remind me that Jacob had died thirteen years before I was born. That silenced me until—months or even years later—I tried again. My father never understood my insistence upon a visit that could not have occurred. And I remained puzzled, and hurt, by his denial of an encounter that was deeply etched in my memory.

My father and I were both right. Jacob may have died long before he came to see me, but his visit was as real as anything in my childhood. It simply made no sense to me that my own grandfather, after whom I was named, would vanish forever before we even met. I made my peace with adult reality, but I refused to relinquish the wish for Jacob that my memory of his visit so wistfully expressed.

I might have asked my grandmother Minnie, Jacob's widow, about my absent grandfather. As a young boy I knew her slightly from our occasional visits to Pittsburgh (an overnight train ride from New York) during the last years of her life. By then, she was a tiny, wrinkled woman, her white hair pulled back into a tight bun. Once we stayed in her small apartment, where she spoke to me incomprehensibly in Yiddish. The next time, after she had moved in with my father's brother and his family, she was completely withdrawn, a spectral presence burdened by age, memory, and sorrow. We viewed each other warily and silently. The last time, in a nursing home after her leg had been amputated, I was too terrified for anything but a glimpse of her, by then a tiny, broken bird, staring soundlessly, awaiting the imminent end.

Like my grandparents, all my elderly American aunts and uncles were immigrants from Russia or Romania. The women, vivacious and ample, wore their long hair in elaborately braided buns and cooked the same indigestible dinners. The men, stolid and bald, always seemed most relaxed in their suspenders, suit jackets, and watch chains. Their names, like their overstuffed, airless apartments, were virtually identical. Anna and Sam, who owned a small drug store in Philadelphia, were known by the family name "Winokur," to distinguish them from her brother Sam, whose sister Annette, with her husband Morris, owned a small laundry on West 111th Street, literally in the shadow of the massive St. John's Cathedral. Looming across Amsterdam Avenue, it was a forbidding fortress of Catholicism which, in my childhood imagination, menaced our entire family.

Not only were my relatives generationally distant; they were culturally foreign. Just how foreign I learned during a shared moment of family trauma, late in World War II. My mother's brother had just been drafted into the army. Our extended family gathered in my grandmother's living room in Philadelphia to lament his fate. (And, I subsequently learned, to berate the Christian neighbors whose irritation with his draft-exempt status had prompted the local draft board to reassess his deferment.) After some hushed conversation over tea, brewed in the Russian samovar that was the family icon of my childhood, my grandmother and her sisters, spontaneously returning to the Odessa they had left behind as young girls, suddenly burst into tears and began to shriek and wail in Yiddish.

I was stunned by their outpouring. I had never seen adults cry. The few cryptic Yiddish expressions I knew were reserved to conceal privileged information from my ears, or to admonish an intrusive relative to leave me alone. This outburst was extraordinary, an expression of primal fear as though my uncle was about to be impressed into the czar's army. No less startling than their volubility was my parents' controlled silence. A generation further along in the Americanization process, they stoically accepted what provoked terror in their elders, still haunted by old country fears. The language of silence, like Yiddish, had meanings that I could not yet fathom.

There was an apt childhood metaphor for the barrier that separated my family from our Jewish origins in Eastern Europe. It was our living-room wall, which we shared with neighbors in the adjacent apartment. In our small building in Queens, where we moved when I was five, voices always carried through walls and across the narrow courtyard. I knew the downstairs voice of maternal supervision, always shrill, admonishing my friend or his sister for their transgressions, real or imagined. And the courtyard voice, a soprano of aspiring culture, incessantly trilling musical scales in pursuit of operatic stardom. But the voice on the other side of our living room wall was unmistakably Jewish. I heard it constantly throughout my childhood. Splendidly cantorial, it was vibrant with words I did not understand and with melodies I could not elude.

I rarely saw our neighbor, Cantor Gorsky, a plump, clean-shaven, middle-aged man who, like my father, always wore a fedora. But I often heard him. Several afternoons each week, while I did my homework on the other side of the wall, he prepared neighborhood boys for their bar mitzvahs. I was a captive audience, inadvertently learning the *Haftarah* blessings long before it was my turn to cross the boundary that separated us.

Although the Sabbath bride never visited our family, Cantor Gorsky hovered nearby every Friday night. Nothing changed in our home, but Cantor Gorsky was an audible presence at our dinner table. His disembodied voice recited *kiddush* over our glasses of water; said the *motzi* over our whole wheat bread; and welcomed the Sabbath with song and prayer that resounded through our little dinette. It seemed perfectly normal to hear Cantor Gorsky sing while my parents conversed, their words and his melodies floating past me in American and Jewish orbits of sound.

But it was hard for me to imagine that Judaism was worth singing about, so warily did my parents avoid contact with it. They must have been astonished, even dismayed, after our move to discover that their nearest neighbor was so identifiably Jewish. Throughout my boyhood, the wall that divided our apartments partitioned Judaism. I was always apprehensive lest any transgression of our mutual boundary entrap me in some unimaginable thicket of Jewish ritual.

I worried needlessly, for baseball had already begun to envelop me in its daily drama, statistical minutiae, and wholesome American distractions. My father gained momentary luster when he shared some memories of Honus Wagner, the great Pittsburgh star whose exploits were well known to me. Otherwise, baseball was entirely my world. Yet in our second-generation family, even baseball activated deeply embedded Jewish ambiguities.

I was astonished to discover, one September morning when I was nine years old, that fame had touched my quite ordinary family. Every newspaper carried the identical picture of a jubilant baseball player crossing home plate after his stunning, ninth-inning, pennant-winning, grand-slam home run in the final game of the season. In as miraculous a revelation as my childhood permitted, I learned that Hank Greenberg of the Detroit Tigers was my cousin.

Only many years later did I realize that Hank was not only my personal hero, but a legendary figure to an entire generation of American Jews. The very idea of a Jewish baseball star, who not only had the chutzpah to challenge Babe Ruth's home run record but who declined to play on the Jewish holy days, fired many more imaginations than mine. Even more than his slugging, Hank's momentous decision to elevate Judaism above baseball was a memorable staple of our family's oral tradition.

Although it made no sense to me that anyone would decline to play baseball at any time, for any reason, those periodic references to Hank's abstinence, more than a decade earlier, left a deep impression. So did his patriotic loyalty, for he had enlisted in the military before the United States was an active belligerent in World War II and he was the first major-leaguer to volunteer after Pearl Harbor. I did not wonder, at the time, whether we revered Hank because he was so genuinely Jewish, so patriotically American, or (as I subsequently learned) so profoundly ambivalent.

It was more than sufficient that he belonged to us, lifting our family from obscurity. Once, during his final season as a Tiger (1946), he even left tickets for my father and me at the Yankee Stadium box office. I spent the entire afternoon gazing in awe at the "5" on his back, just a few yards from where we sat. Even if no one but my father could recall precisely whose cousin was whose, back in Romania, there was no doubt about the family connection. I treasured it.

Many years later, I was surprised to learn that the familiar story of Hank's Jewish observance had been conveniently altered in the family retelling. The facts were indisputable: in 1934, as the Detroit Tigers neared their first pennant in twenty-five years, Hank was indeed caught between conflicting obligations to Judaism and to his team. Under the glare of intense press scrutiny, which displayed evident bewilderment that a sane person might experience conflict between a pennant race and anything else, no less religion, Hank had consulted the chief rabbi of Detroit.

While Jewish religious obligation indeed mandated observance, the rabbi conceded that Hank also had to consider his civic duty. The rabbi, the better to escape the horns of his own loyalty dilemma, shifted the burden. Hank, as "a conscientious Jew, must decide for himself whether he ought to play or not." Given such delphic rabbinical pronouncements, it was hardly surprising that one Detroit newspaper proclaimed: "Talmud Clears Greenberg for Holiday Play."

Hank, encouraged by the rabbi to be a good American and decide for himself, resolved his conundrum by attending Rosh ha-Shanah services in the morning, hitting two home runs in the afternoon (in a crucial game that Detroit won, 2–1), and, with the pennant race all but over, sitting out the game on Yom Kippur ten days later. His decision not to choose between uncomfortable alternatives but to embrace every possibility was—for his generation of American Jews—perfect. Playing when necessary and observing when convenient, he emphatically affirmed his commitment as a team player without diminishing his identity as a Jew. Like the biblical Jacob, he wrestled with his conscience, but like any normal American boy, he picked up his bat and played the game.

Hank's stardom demonstrated that despite religious impediments (for Judaism never seemed in any way advantageous to me), a Jew could join the "American" team. Talent and perseverance assured his place in the clubhouse among the *goyim*, where Jews yearned to be. Whether in the uniform of a Detroit Tiger or a Flying Tiger, Hank was a Jew who expressed abiding loyalty to American ideals.

Hank was my unrivaled boyhood hero. Not because he agonized over Jewish issues, but because he hit home runs. He also left a deep impression for another reason. In 1947, his last season as a player, Jackie Robinson shattered baseball's racial barrier. Hank offered solace and encouragement to Robinson at a difficult time. In a marvelous moment of interracial compassion, the former butt of anti-Semitic taunts stood by another victim of racism. Quietly but unmistakably, Hank identified the common struggle of Jews and Negroes to realize the promise of American democracy.

Hank's compassion (and the ineptitude of his new team, the Pittsburgh Pirates) prompted the transfer of my baseball loyalties to the Brooklyn Dodgers, Robinson's team. Unlike the Yankees, whose very name (along with the arrogance that accompanied their incessant victories) made them anathema, the Dodgers symbolized my unconscious ideal: the American melting pot. Robinson joined a team that soon included Southern gentlemen (Pee Wee Reese), hillbillies (Preacher Roe), Italians (Carl Furillo), Poles (Andy Pafko), aristocrats (Duke Snider), and Jews (Cal Abrams). Southern racists (Dixie Walker) who opposed Robinson's presence were quickly traded away. In becoming a Dodger fan, I affirmed my commitment to American opportunity and equality. I knew that Hank would be proud of me.

In my family, the only public figure whose stature equalled Hank's was Franklin D. Roosevelt. Nor was that unusual, for no group of Americans bestowed more lavish affection upon Roosevelt than second-generation American Jews. My parents were thoroughly apolitical. I knew nothing of social security or bank deposit insurance. But even though, by a narrow margin of comfort, we were not among the one-third of the nation described by Roosevelt as ill-fed, ill-clothed, and ill-housed, our family adoration of Roosevelt was undisguised. The Hyde Park aristocrat was our liberal benefactor. His patrician benevolence helped wash away some of the lingering stigma of our immigrant origins, assuring people like my parents that they were genuinely American.

As much as I treasured Hank Greenberg's autograph, I also prized my letter, on White House stationary, thanking me for asking the President to purchase a war bond in our school bond drive. Still, I was astonished when my mother dragged me, in a pouring rain, to cheer the Roosevelt motorcade as it raced along Queens Boulevard during the 1944 presidential campaign. I did not see Roosevelt, but I did catch a glimpse of his dog, Fala. Just six months later, Roosevelt's death was a genuine family tragedy. My parents and grandmother huddled around our radio in shocked and tearful disbelief. I had simply assumed that Roosevelt always would be president, as during my lifetime he always had been.

My parents' boundless adulation for Roosevelt was unexceptional. If, among family or friends, there lurked a Republican, it was as carefully guarded a secret as the shameful conviction of a distant relative for tax evasion. I assumed that we loved Roosevelt because he was so good, his compassion for forgotten Americans embracing us within the American family. How could American Jews not revere the president who stocked the arsenal of democracy to wage war against Hitler? I knew nothing of his indifference to the plight of European Jewry before or during the Holocaust. That has never diminished the unrequited love that American Jews bestowed upon him, then or since.

My parents purchased their ticket of admission to American society with silence on any public issue involving Jews. Not a word was ever spoken about the Holocaust, even though several of my father's aunts (Jacob's sisters) remained in Romania. Perhaps Romania's wartime alliance with Nazi Germany made any expression of concern suspect. A fervent patriot, my father took whatever meager savings he managed to accumulate and dutifully bought government war bonds. He thereby lost the opportunity seized by a cousin or two to invest in the stock market and profit handsomely from the postwar economic boom.

Too old for the draft, my father became an auxiliary fireman instead, proudly setting forth on weekends with his helmet and armband to learn first aid and fire-fighting techniques. My mother did her part for the war effort by hoarding food rationing stamps, which enabled her to buy under-the-counter lamb chops from our profiteering butcher. My primary role in the war, besides collecting tin foil, was studying the silouettes of German war planes, the better to identify them should they ever appear in the skies over Forest Hills.

With my father as my salesman, I also sold more war bonds than anyone else in my grammar school. That entitled me to have my picture taken for the local newspaper with our school principal, a dour and sour Irish lady who clearly was uncomfortable with the marketing skills of her Jewish pupils. We all took air-raid drills seriously; and we expected Nazi spies to arrive by submarine momentarily. My friends and I stocked our basement hideout with enough comic books and bubble gum for any emergency.

As the war in Europe ended, I learned about Buchenwald and Dachau from *Life* magazine. Except for the "March of Time" newsreels that supplemented our movie matinee double features, *Life* provided my only glimpses of the outside world. (The radio was largely reserved for classical music, soap operas, and The Lone Ranger.) I was riveted by the pictures of hideously emaciated survivors, the stacks of naked bodies, the gas chambers and ovens. For weeks, I returned to stare at the photographs, too terrified to ask any questions. My parents, who read *Life* faithfully, said nothing. I searched the faces of the "good" Germans who were taken to witness the mass graves adjacent to their homes and fields, of which they claimed blissful ignorance. Perhaps I sensed the presence of my parents, other Americans, all adults, among them.

I learned still more from the Nuremberg war-crime trials, which I followed avidly. Hitler and Goebbels were already dead by suicide, but the names of the Nazi criminals formed my All-Star team of evil, and I never forgot them: Göring, Hess, von Ribbentrop, Jodl, and Seyss-Inquart, among others. During my early teens, when the first survivor memoirs and atrocity studies were published, I discovered a friend with whom to share my obsessive fascination with Josef Mengele's maniacal medical experiments on twin children and the lamp shades made by Ilsa Koch from human skin. We traded horror stories culled from our reading, as if to immunize ourselves against our deepest fears. We even experimented to discover whether we could have held our breath long enough to have survived the gas chambers.

My parents, keeping their silence on Jewish subjects, said as little about miracles as about catastrophes. They were not Zionists; Jewish nationalism must have seemed too risky a commitment for patriotic American Jews. In their own way, they preserved the carefully calibrated duality that was their American Jewish hallmark. But my mother, momentarily inspired by the passionate Zionist oratory of Rabbi Stephen S. Wise, joined Hadassah, the better to attend Manhattan luncheons where he was the featured speaker. She raved about his magnetism, but nothing was ever said at home about the Jewish struggle for national independence.

Even in Hebrew school, where I suffered two afternoons and one Sunday morning every week for four years, the struggle for Jewish statehood, which culminated the year before my bar mitzvah, was largely ignored. Hebrew school was not a place of learning; it was merely part of a tacit bargain with our parents. We accepted temporary Jewish confinement for the promise of future American freedom. I experienced Hebrew school and the diluted Judaism it struggled to transmit as the bitter medicine in my otherwise healthy life. Like all my fellow-suffering friends, I grimaced and swallowed it reluctantly. In retribution, I tormented my harried teachers and yearned for my bar mitzvah when I finally would be pronounced cured of the debilitating malady for which Hebrew school was prescribed.

My parents constantly played out their own interior family drama of Jewish identity and evasion. My mother denigrated my father's "lower class" (translated, Orthodox) origins. Our every trip to Brooklyn or the Bronx to visit his brother and sister became a downward descent back to the shtetl. Her parents' Odessa certainly was more cosmopolitan than Jacob's Bostosoni; and their Bund socialism more sophisticated than his Orthodoxy. But any social distinction between her father the tailor and his father the teamster was probably indiscernible.

My mother had been scarred during her girlhood years by the anti-Semitic prejudice, laced with class arrogance, that she encountered in Philadelphia. My father's extended family bore the brunt of her resentment, for she equated Jewishness with cultural deprivation. In our triangular interactions (I was the only child), I was trapped between my father's devotion to family and my mother's discomfort with it. Either choice, of course, compelled me to reject one of my parents.

My father, undeterred by my mother's scorn, began a quiet postwar search for survivors from Jacob's Romanian family. He placed inquiries in the European Jewish press and by some incredible coincidence a member of his family actually responded. For many years thereafter, my father sent money and clothing to family members whom he had never seen, first in Romania and then, after his aunts and their children were released from British internment camps on Cyprus, in Israel.

Slowly, a correspondence with his cousin Minna began to reconnect the remnants of his family, scattered by war and wandering. Each envelope that arrived from abroad, its elaborate script nearly obliterated by the profusion of stamps, tantalized me. To whom were we bound so closely, at such a distance? And why? Those letters must have gratified my father. But he remained silent about his righteous deeds for nearly twenty years. I finally learned about them when he made his first and only trip to Israel, where he presided over a joyous family reunion with relatives who revered him as their American benefactor.

After seven years of silent auditing, I finally crossed the barrier that separated Cantor Gorsky's apartment from ours. How strange it felt to be sitting on the other side of the wall, in the presence of the magisterial voice that I had heard for so long. I assumed that our curious relationship was shared. But Cantor Gorsky seemed oblivious. I was merely another boy in the endless procession of students who came to him to be taught what they did not want to learn. For all of us, normal life was suspended during our year with him. It was not quite as bad as orthodonture, but it was not appreciably better.

I felt overwhelmed by Cantor Gorsky's mastery of this mysterious Jewish world of language and ritual that I was now expected to enter. But why this ordeal, so vital yet so irrelevant? I could not begin to understand that the mixed message answered itself. This rite of passage to adult membership in the community of Jews was, in my family circle, the exit from Judaism. It was as though my parents had learned a garbled version of the traditional prayer that released the father of a bar mitzvah boy from responsibility for his son's deeds and misdeeds. In their American rendition, the bar mitzvah released the son from any further obligation to be a Jew. Cantor Gorsky presided over our transition to Americanism: he certified us as Jews as we departed from Judaism.

My bar mitzvah, elaborately choreographed by my parents, emphatically affirmed the contradiction. During Friday evening and Saturday morning services, the Jewish religious formalities were observed. Cantor Gorsky had prepared me well. My flawless singing, in a voice as yet unchanged, was matched only by my ignorance of what it all meant, or why I was doing it. Indeed, it was the only time in my life that my parents and I ever sat together in a synagogue. I am certain that my father was proud of me but on this subject, as on so many others, he could not easily articulate his feelings.

Shortly before my momentous day, however, he had accompanied me on a remarkable journey to the Lower East Side. It was as close to ritual as he ever came. Although the Lower East Side was no longer *the* authentic Jewish residential neighborhood of New York, stores along Hester and Essex Streets were still stocked with prayer books and ceremonial objects. We walked by them, gingerly navigating our way around barrels filled with pickles and shmaltz herring. To my astonishment, my father knew exactly where to take me to buy my blue and white *tallit* and my satin *yarmulka*. It was the only boyhood glimpse I ever had of the world of his childhood, and the only intimation that he still knew where to find it.

But he left me to venture alone, during the week preceding my bar mitzvah, to a shabby upstairs room in the synagogue previously unknown to me. There, a *minyan* of elderly men, as eager to socialize as to pray, came for early morning services. We students knew the downstairs, where we tumbled out of classes and shouted in the hallways. Upstairs was different; it actually seemed Jewish. I was terrified.

These old men offered a glimpse of a Jewish world that I hardly knew existed and certainly wanted nothing to do with. They barely acknowledged my presence, although one of them kindly helped me to untangle my *t'fillin*. Called to the *bima* in a rehearsal for my bar mitzvah, I felt suffocated by the wizened men who hovered around me, and dizzied by the Hebrew words that floated up from the enormous Torah scroll. My discomfort was abetted by Cantor Gorsky's sharply whispered rebuke when I forgot to repeat a response to one of the blessings. But I had to do it alone, for my father's decision that my bar mitzvah was mandatory implied nothing by way of his own participation.

The ceremony itself was a hazy blur, but the festivities that followed remained a vivid embarassment. My bar mitzvah was the necessary prelude to an ostentatious parental assertion of family status. From the synagogue in Forest Hills we traveled in a cortege of cars (appropriately funereal) to the acme of my mother's yearnings: to Manhattan, then to Park Avenue, and finally to our destination at the Waldorf-Astoria hotel.

There, in two large banquet rooms, I was immediately swallowed up in crowds of family, friends, and business associates who had been invited to witness and certify our social ascent. We might still be mired in a $79-a-month rented apartment in Queens, but Manhattan was our destination. I was too young to comprehend the social strivings of second-generation American Jews. But I was old enough to detect Jewish hypocrisy. The next morning, declaring my own priorities (now that I was entitled by Jewish tradition to assert them), I left the hotel to return alone by subway to Forest Hills, to watch the Dodgers' game on our new television set.

The boundaries of my childhood world seldom extended very far beyond the subway line that linked Queens to Manhattan. Pittsburgh, where my father's family lived, was remote. But Philadelphia, where my adoring maternal grandmother owned a small drug store and soda fountain, was paradise. There, my deepest cravings were sated. Early in the morning, I raced downstairs to help her open the store, where I was permitted to sell penny candy to envious neighborhood children. At the end of the day, my reward was an ice-cream soda made to my own recipe. My granny was the source of my sweetest childhood nourishment; ice cream was the least of it.

We also traveled occasionally to Brooklyn or the Bronx. But these neighborhoods, to say nothing of my father's relatives, aroused my mother's snobbery. She preferred vacations in Atlantic City with hotels, restaurants, and hired help (the more obsequious the better). Once we even joined the extended Greenberg family in Long Branch, where, during an hour of unmitigated euphoria, my cousins and I chased fly balls that Hank hit to us, while visions of his instant recognition of my fielding skills (sadly, quite limited) danced in my head.

A different realm of fantasy, one with rustic New England charm, was provided by my mother's cousin. Jen, a free spirit in her college days in Madison (where she had met her husband Karl), was the family bohemian. Old photos revealed her scantily clothed in diaphanous gowns (in the fashion of Isadora Duncan), dancing with her girl friends in the sylvan woods along the shore of Lake Mendota. I yearned for that freedom, and more.

When I met them, Jen and Karl were struggling to realize his vision of owning an old-fashioned country store in New England. They had purchased a ramshackle eighteenth-century farmhouse near Great Barrington, which they renovated during weekend visits from Brooklyn. It astonished me that anyone in our family would choose to live outside of the city, especially in a house at the bottom of a dirt road by a stream, nestled in the Berkshire hills. There was even a dog, a bouncy terrier named Val. No one I knew owned a dog, or even a cat. Among my friends, confined as we all were to small apartments, the limited possibilities were defined by tropical fish and turtles.

My summer camp was located nearby, so we squeezed in occasional visits, although neither of my parents cared for grass or bugs. But I was thoroughly enchanted by the rustic surroundings, working fireplaces, a vast assortment of pewter pitchers and bowls in the dining room hutch and, on a wall near their four-poster bed, Karl's eccentric collection of pocket watches, ticking and ringing unharmoniously. Karl had a puckish sense of humor that was all but unknown in my family, and Jen's expansive warmth contrasted with my mother's self-absorption.

I secretly declared them my surrogate parents. I was as enraptured as they were with their colonial American fantasies. When I was a teenager, my parents permitted me to travel alone by train to Great Barrington for visits. I made the trip several times and its magic never receded. I loved to watch the conductor swing down the aisle punching tickets, angling them into a metal slot at each seat, calling out the litany of local stops: Kent, Wallingford, Gaylordsville, New Milford, finally Canaan, the last stop in Connecticut.

It was pitch dark and bitter cold when we reached the Great Barrington station. Karl, usually accompanied by his young sons, met the train to drive me home. The fireplaces were always aglow, and Jen had hot chocolate waiting. Exhausted and exhilarated, I slept deeply and awoke early, feeling the morning chill seep through the house. After the boys went off to school, Jen and I ate breakfast together. Her dark eyes and long braids evoked memories of my grandmother, the only other generously loving woman in our family. By 7:30, Jen was already drinking her third cup of coffee and smoking her third cigarette and was ready to talk. Although I cannot recall ever discussing anything but baseball with adults, Jen was different. We talked until she was ready to leave for the store.

Sometimes I accompanied her, spending the morning wandering around the cavernous barn that Karl had converted into a faithful replica of a colonial village. My favorite place (and, I suspect, his) was the old-fashioned candy store, stocked with jars of peppermint sticks and sour balls, stacks of fudge, and packages of locally baked ginger-molasses cookies, whose recipe remained a carefully guarded secret known only to him. Karl always gave me my own paper bag, which I filled to overflowing. When the sweet abundance of it all finally overwhelmed me, I retreated behind a secret door to his office to read quietly, devour my goodies, and recall similar indulgences at my grandmother's soda fountain.

Often I remained behind, alone in the house. My favorite room was the rear parlor. It was lined with books donated by my uncle, an eccentric bachelor who roamed the world on a succession of business ventures that took him through Europe and Africa. His library was an enticing collection of literature from the 1920s, and I delighted in it. There was a hi-fi and stacks of records. I always celebrated my return by listening to the Weavers and Theodore Bikel.

In the evenings, we drank tea together by the fire. A group of their friends often came by. A stellar gathering of local celebrities, it usually included the taciturn psychologist Erik Erikson and Artie Shaw, the ebullient band leader. When the conversation edged into sophistication or bombast and exceeded my powers of participation, I lapsed into silence, fascinated and overwhelmed in roughly equivalent measure.

A few days in the Berkshires with Jen and Karl reinforced all my Norman Rockwell images of true Americanism: an old house in the New England woods filled with books and fireplaces and children. Even the dog and cat were mutually affectionate. Jen's warmth and Karl's wit, her skill at driving a car and his at riding a horse, were attributes unknown in my family. Long before I could identify their dream of acculturation I was inspired by it, for it seemed genuinely wholesome in a way that my parents' material strivings never did. Yet even in this fantasy family, there was the familiar silent drama of Jewish ambiguity. Unlike his brother, who had changed the family name, Karl kept his, choosing to remain a Brooklyn Jew even as he reinvented himself as a colonial New Englander.

But it was Forest Hills, for the most part, that defined the cultural boundaries of my world. We lived at the end of a long block of attached row houses, in a low apartment building with perhaps thirty other families. Ours were the only apartments in a neighborhood of private homes, bounded by the aristocratic West Side Tennis Club at one end and the Forest Hills Jewish Center at the other. The adjacent streets were alphabetically arranged, with an English lilt: Dartmouth, Exeter, Fleet, Groton, and Harrow. Our neighbors, Cantor Gorsky excepted, were remarkably like us, in transit from immigrant Judaism to American respectability.

The public school across the street was almost as Jewish as my Hebrew school. But the Board of Education still had difficulty certifying anyone with a "Jewish" accent, so most of our teachers were Irish. They were inclined to behave like British colonial officers, dispatched to remote outposts to "civilize" the natives. The nearest stores—two drug stores, a small grocery, and the dry cleaner—

were all owned by Jews. Even Jack, the vegetable man, was Jewish. Surrounded by Jews, my friends and I took being Jewish for granted, as long as no Jewish content intruded to spoil the identification.

Jewish holidays came and went, unobserved if not entirely unnoticed. I am certain my father always knew but he never let on. The closest he ever came to a principled position on the subject was his firm refusal, one December, to satisfy my yearning for a Christmas tree. But on Christmas morning, there were always presents. Christmas was a strange day in our family, since my mother, who had been born on December 25, celebrated her birthday a month later because her parents had not wanted their daughter to bear any Christian taint. While I opened my Christmas presents, we tiptoed silently around her Christmas birthday.

Except in Hebrew school and at occasional but interminable Passover Seders with Greenberg relatives, I encountered Jewish ritual only once in my childhood. Bobby, who lived nearby, never belonged to our apartment-house gang but he was occasionally included, especially when we needed a scapegoat. For some incomprehensible reason, during the week following his father's funeral when his family sat *shiva*, I visited his house. I had never been there before, and I felt instantly that I should not be there then.

According to Orthodox custom, all the mirrors were draped. A memorial candle flickered in the shadowy gloom. There were low benches for the mourners, and soft cushions had been removed from the sofa. In our family, death was never even discussed. Older relatives simply disappeared; only months later might their fate be noted. (I knew by my mother's screams when my granny died, but I was not permitted to attend her funeral.) In Bobby's house, I felt suffocated by the symbols of death. I left quickly and never returned. When I heard, just a few years later, that Bobby himself was dying of leukemia, it seemed to confirm the strangeness of his life without a father or, now, even a future.

Religious symbols of any sort had enormous power to frighten me. Among our grammar-school expeditions to the Museum of Natural History and the New York Public Library was a visit to St. Patrick's Cathedral. This immense gothic structure consumed an entire city block in midtown Manhattan. I was too young, as a

fourth grader, to have learned anything about the separation of religion and state, but I knew that a church, especially if it was
Catholic, was forbidden territory even to the most marginal of Jews.
Inside the massive front portals (the better to trap me, I feared),
I was terrified. The further we ventured, the more claustrophobic
I felt. I was startled by a life-size effigy, dressed in full church
regalia, enclosed in glass. Whether it was a saint or a pope hardly
mattered; whoever it was certainly would know that I was Jewish
and punish me for trespassing. Dozens of thin, tapered candles
flickered in neat rows; there was a pervasive odor of incense. Little
gnomes in black dresses and shawls flitted about like sparrows,
knelt, and crossed themselves. Men in long robes and starched
collars, droning in a strange language, were addressed as "Father."
I must have realized that there were some definitive boundaries
after all, neither as camouflaged nor as permeable as I had assumed.
I would cross them at my peril. I still cannot walk past St. Patrick's
without reliving that childhood apprehension.

I had not yet learned how carefully my father navigated our
family around such hazards. Forest Hills was certifiably Jewish territory, long before Israelis flocked to the new high-rise apartment
buildings on the far side of Queens Boulevard. So, too, was his
office on West 34th Street, in the shadow of the Empire State building. Ever since our move from Philadelphia when I was two years
old, he had worked as a salesman for a large costume jewelry company. Its name, Coro (for its founders, Cohen and Rosenberger),
reflected the anxieties that beset my father's generation of Jews.
The confident, successful (and thoroughly assimilated) German
Jewish merchants of the nineteenth century were eager to proclaim
their names on their businesses: Gimbel, Bloomingdale, Levi
Strauss. They emulated the assertive self-promotion of Yankees like
Henry Ford or Louis Tiffany. But the new immigrants from Eastern
Europe who followed them were far more apprehensive and re-
strained. Safe passage, not instant recognition, was their goal. Who
could ever identify the owners of Coro from its name?
The world of costume jewelry was far removed from my most
peripheral boyhood concerns, but I loved to accompany my father
to his office even though I could never figure out exactly what he

did there. He proudly displayed me to the receptionist, to other salesmen, and, occasionally and with exceeding deference, to "old Mr. Rosenberger," as the owner was respectfully known. I played happily at his desk, in the salesmen's back room, far from the glitter of Coro rhinestones on conspicuous display in the lobby.

His office buddies, from the same American Jewish mold, were also married men in their early forties with young children. They bantered easily with one another and graciously admired my father's prize bauble, as he would theirs. He felt appreciated there, and he clearly enjoyed the male camaraderie. I doubt that he ever questioned the value of selling costume jewelry to stores that enticed middle-class women who were striving, as was my mother, to appear fashionable. It was his job and, given his memories of the Depression, he could only have been grateful for it.

Not long after my bar mitzvah, however, his status at Coro abruptly changed. All that I learned from many whispered conversations was that the assurance of his steady, if modest, salary, soon would yield to the precarious uncertainty of sales commissions. Anything that evoked memories of his own childhood financial insecurity must have filled my father with dread. I could sense his suffering only dimly for, like everything else of importance, it was never discussed in my presence. But it surfaced, painfully, after my parents saw Arthur Miller's *Death of a Salesman*, a brutal public confirmation to my father of his own vulnerability. He identified completely with Willy Loman: so eager to be well-liked, so dependent upon the good will of others, so susceptible to his own illusions. I suspect that he feared the financial disaster and ultimate shame that was Willy's fate.

Yet, in a miraculous inversion, real life provided a happy twist to theatrical melodrama. A cousin's business partner suddenly died, and my father was invited to buy his share of a small jewelry manufacturing company located in the pulsating hub of the diamond district on West 47th Street. My father agonized. A higher salary and the glimmer of future affluence cost dearly. He had to invest his entire life savings and borrow an equivalent amount from his brother, Harry, to transform himself from a salesman to a businessman.

It took both desperation and courage for my father, nearing fifty and facing at least a decade of debt before he could even begin to replenish his own depleted financial resources, to seize the opportunity. My mother pressured him relentlessly to do it. She knew that a business partnership (with Hank Greenberg's brother, no less) could propel us decisively up the ladder of social mobility. So, from Coro, my father moved to Ide, its name an acronym from the initials of its founders, Isenberg, Dubin, and Ehrenreich.

My mother's judgment was unerring. Within a year or two, we had abandoned Forest Hills for the Upper East Side of Manhattan. My parents joined a country club in New Jersey. Now we ate our Sunday evening dinners at Lindy's, the popular tourist and celebrity mecca on Broadway, rather than at Topsy's, the Queens Boulevard chicken restaurant. It was indeed a rapid ascent, if within a rather narrow range. But I never lost my embarrassment that my father's new health-club membership propelled us inside Lindy's to the head of the line, past the crowds of less-privileged tourists shivering outside in the cold. My self-imposed punishment, to my parents' bewildered consternation, was to deny myself a slice of Lindy's famous cheesecake.

To earn these luxuries, my father traveled with grim determination. He imposed upon himself a repayment schedule to his brother as rigid as any bank would have demanded. Harry had answered my father's hesitant inquiry about a loan of thirty thousand dollars with the instant pledge, "You've got it." For the first time ever, I saw my father cry. He dutifully mailed monthly payments to Pittsburgh, carefully deducting each one from the balance that he maintained in a little notebook that he always carried with him.

His prolonged absences on business trips—four times each year for as long as six weeks, with frequent shorter trips—were a continuous reminder of the financial sword of Damocles that hung over our family. I memorized his itinerary, from Chicago through Houston, along the west coast from Los Angeles to Seattle, and back east through Salt Lake City and Denver. In his endless cross-country meanderings, Pittsburgh always was the last, and surely the best, stop before he returned to New York. Everywhere else meant hotels; but in Pittsburgh he returned to his true home and family. There, far more than in Forest Hills, he was loved and appreciated. I learned to rely upon his trips to mend the frayed fabric of family memory. I depended on him, almost against my will, to convey news of graduations and engagements, weddings and births, triumphs and sorrows. My father linked us together even as we were growing further apart.

Many years later, my cousin Sondra recalled the eager anticipation that framed his visits to Pittsburgh. Not only did she and her sisters imagine that my father resembled Cary Grant, they knew that his love for them was overflowing. "We hovered around him and his treasure, everything asparkle," she remembered: "our eyes, his eyes watching us, the ruby eyes of rhinestone turtles, golden bumble bees"—all carefully chosen to delight them. In Pittsburgh, and only there, could he savor the joy of family affection.

My father's new office was on a high floor of a building whose tenants all sold gold and platinum jewelry adorned with diamonds. West 47th Street, between Fifth and Sixth Avenues, was (and is) a teeming hive of buyers and sellers, a tumultuous open-air and closed-door market that might have been transplanted intact from Eastern Europe. The diamond industry was subdivided between Hasidic Jews (whose full beards, dark hats, and Yiddish fluency violated every norm of Jewish propriety that I knew) and second-generation Americans like my father, identifiable by their clean-shaven faces, gray fedoras, and slightly more comprehensible English.

Amid the noisy bustle of this Jewish male enclave (the only women were customers), diamonds were scrutinized through jeweler's loupes, stones and rings changed hands in tiny manila envelopes, and hundred-dollar bills were more commonplace than fives or tens. Pockets emptied of cash were filled with diamonds, and—as Molly Goldberg would say on my father's favorite television program—versa visa. The world was viewed through facets and measured in carats. The language of the street, whether Yiddish or English, was cryptic. I never heard a complete sentence.

Diamonds, according to industry advertisements, were forever. Selling them, however, was frenetic. On West 47th Street no one walked, talked, or ate slowly. There was a palpable, manic energy, edged by an anxiety for deals to be completed quickly lest a calamity erupt. It was easy to imagine some undefined but menacing tremor that would empty the street of people as instantly as when its flocks of resident pigeons would take startled flight. The diamond business, historically, was perfectly suited to Jews, who could pocket all their assets at the first rumble of a pogrom and flee for their lives, to prosper another day in a different place.

Occasionally, after a frenzied twenty-minute lunch in a local delicatessen where the size of the portions presupposed the imminence of famine, I accompanied my father to one of the huge diamond arcades. Surrounded by display cases filled with shining gold and glistening stones, I always felt overwhelmed by the vulgarity of it all. So many people thrashing about in the same stocked pool of avarice. Yet I could not, despite myself, avoid respecting these businessmen, whose shared bonds of trust enabled my father to depart with thousands of dollars of jewels—"on consignment" in the magic phrase—without a deposit or even a receipt.

Inside my father's office, past the locked security door, the din was unremitting. The partners, like most spouses I knew, hollered at each other incessantly, their voices reverberating through rooms stripped of everything but bare essentials: desks, chairs, files, and a huge safe with multiple dials, wheels, and handles. An old oak time-punch clock ticked loudly in the background. Unlike everything else on West 47th Street, it was always slow.

The large rear room was the "factory," where a dozen or so skilled workers plied their craft. They sweltered together at long benches, winter and summer alike, for the radiators could not be adjusted and it never occurred to the partners that anyone was entitled to be comfortable. The craftsmen were said to be well paid, with a union to protect them; that was sufficient. After every visit, as the balky elevator jerked its way down to street level, I exulted that I had eluded the career trap that my father had set for me.

Visits to my father's office were an occasional diversion, but the formative institutions of my boyhood were summer camp and private school. I spent my first summer at Camp Greylock in the Berkshires at the age of eight. For the next decade, it provided a two-month idyll every summer. There, I was surrounded by boys who only wanted, as did I, an endless round of vigorously competitive sports without parents, girls, homework, or other irritating distractions.

The camp was venerable and respected, even dynastic. It had always been owned by a family of four brothers, whose complementary personalities symbolized the harmonious reconciliation of nature, competition, spirituality, and profit. The guiding ideologue was an eccentric high-school principal from Brooklyn, known to everyone as "Doc." His major contribution, every Friday night, was the attempt to inspire our band of restless hellions to spiritual contemplation. We gathered after sundown around a campfire to sing, laugh, cheer, and endure Doc's abstruse musings about eternity, our souls, and other abstractions that were even less illuminating than the fireflies we tried to capture as he spoke.

Friday evening campfires were barely tolerable diversions from our relentlessly competitive regimen. We came to camp to play baseball and basketball and to win "color war," little else. But the campfires molded us in ways that we could not possibly have understood at the time. All of us, campers and counselors alike, were Jews. Together, we "observed" the Sabbath in our own parody of observance, never permitting anything Jewish to intrude upon our Friday evening ritual. Scrubbed clean, dressed in white, singing together by the fire, we almost precisely replicated the forms of Jewish ritual appropriate to the night while completely expunging them of Jewish substance. For Doc, a lapsed Jew turned Ethical Culturist, there surely was no better time than the Jewish Sabbath to evade our Jewishness.

Jewish acculturation, laced with Jewish ambivalence, was far more subtle at the high school I loved as much as camp. Some of my camp friends attended Horace Mann, a fine private school in New York, and it seemed quite logical to me that I should enjoy the advantages of summer camp—boys and sports—the year around. I persuaded my parents that their dreams for my college education and my dreams for a career with the New York Knicks both hinged upon my transfer there.

I was eager, yet so apprehensive. There I was, a boy from the backwoods of Queens for whom serious reading meant John R.

Tunis or *Life* magazine, about to enter an institution of tradition and culture. The imposing grey stone buildings with their arched enclosures and leaded glass windows evoked the same awed anxiety that once made me so uneasy in St. Patrick's Cathedral. Perhaps I sensed how a secular shrine of learning like Horace Mann might compound the dilemmas of acculturation that tormented second-generation American Jewish families like ours.

My mother, as always, approved any elevation in family status. My father, however, was uneasy. My yearning for Horace Mann, for its seductive invitation to relinquish Jewish parochialism for Western civilization, may have awakened insecurities about his place as a Jew in American society. Certainly, the costs of social striving worried him. Deeply in debt with a new business and a new Manhattan apartment (just across the East River from the Rikers Island prison that he joked would be his punishment for financial failure), he must have wondered when the climbing and acquiring would ever stop. Horace Mann, I assured him, was all that I wanted. He relented.

Once the decision was made, he communicated his anxiety to me in the carefully muted but emotionally laden language of clothing. Always impeccably dressed, my father knew that the right suits, ties, cuff links, and tie clasps could disguise lowly origins. Clothes shopping had always been a wretched experience for me. In my childhood, Lord & Taylor, where the sales people were most officious, was the department store of choice. Under my mother's tutelage, we traveled into Manhattan by subway on Saturday morning to wait interminably among other mothers and sons until it was my turn to be measured, squeezed, and tortured. When I finally rebelled, forcing my father to assume responsibility, we patronized various downtown wholesalers who were recommended by relatives in the garment business. But my father, always a perfectionist about dress, tormented the harried tailors, who retaliated against me with humiliating pinches in sensitive places.

Horace Mann required students to wear jackets and ties. This raised the ante for my father. He cautioned me that many of my new classmates, from families more affluent than ours, could afford expensive clothes that were beyond our means. That was all he said, but his message was clear. Soon enough, precisely as he had anticipated, clothes mattered. After only two days, when I had already depleted my entire wardrobe (except for sweatshirts), I wore a garment made of green corduroy. In my family, it easily qualified as a boy's jacket. At Horace Mann, however, I was informed by the librarian (the designated female monitor of proper dress and clean fingernails) that I was wearing a "shirt," which required a jacket to cover it. I was learning.

My father need not have worried quite so much. Nearly all the boys came from Jewish families on approximately the same rungs of the social-mobility ladder. Most lived in the conventionally fashionable blocks between 80th and 90th Streets, east and west of Central Park. I had a few classmates from the rarified precincts of Park and Fifth Avenues, and, at the other extreme, from the nether realms of Brooklyn and New Jersey. But the handful from wealthy families rarely demonstrated their privilege, and those on scholarship never revealed their hardship. Everyone's father seemed to own a small manufacturing business of some kind; ladies lingerie was especially popular.

Much to the bemusement of our beloved history teacher (who candidly confided his own dream of owning a Cadillac), we all—even the Fifth Avenue boys—resolutely defined ourselves as middle class. Horace Mann, after all, symbolized meritocracy, not aristocracy. The school especially appealed to Eastern European Jewish parents who wanted to propel their sons beyond their own cultural constraints, but not too far or too fast. The children of the German Jewish elite, at least one generation further along in the acculturation process, might attend progressive boarding schools in Vermont, or even Andover or Exeter. Neither we, nor our parents, were prepared for that. Horace Mann, midway between the Flatbush Yeshiva and Groton, was just right.

We were sent to Horace Mann to eradicate any lingering stigma of Jewishness. Traveling by subway, we left the sordid city behind. Not for the Bronx, surely a backward social step; but for its elegant Riverdale neighborhood. There, lawyers and doctors owned fine Tudor and Dutch colonial homes and the spirit of Ethical Culture—symbolized by the liberal Fieldston School—prevailed. As we trudged up the steep incline from 242nd Street to our hilltop haven, our daily ascent affirmed our lowly origins and lofty aspirations.

Horace Mann vigorously asserted its own diluted version of muscular Christianity. Headmasters named Tillinghast and Gratwick and teachers named Williams, Briggs, Farrington, and Crandall, were assigned to instruct six hundred boys named Cohen, Levine, Bernstein, Goldberg, and Rosenthal in the civilized virtues required for adult success. (A few Christian students, mostly the sons of Columbia faculty who recognized a good education when they saw it, comprised the minority at the periphery of each class.) As Jews, we knew that *we* were the real minority, lacking the proper certification for the Gentile world that enticed us. Horace Mann lured us beyond the invisible ghetto walls that still enclosed our parents, funneling us toward the next gateway to status and privilege: the Ivy League.

The school, as my best friend there subsequently entitled his book about the Boy Scout movement, truly was a "character factory." To be sure, we studied history, literature, math, and science in a rigorous regimen that began at 8:30 A.M. and did not end, at least for the athletes among us, until nightfall. But that was the least of it. As our senior yearbook declared portentously, "We entered Horace Mann as boys," and "we hope to graduate as men." As we ascended to masculine maturity, we carefully emulated English public-school students. Dr. Gratwick was the "Headmaster," not the principal (and, with all three buttons of his jacket always buttoned, he certainly looked the part); teachers were addressed as "Sir," not Mr. (unless they were "Coach"); I was not a tenth-grader, but a Fourth Former. The message—rigor shapes character, assuring excellence—was unambiguous.

For the first time, I had friends who took books more seriously than baseball. They jolted me from my torpid indifference toward disciplined study and rigorous learning. Indeed, it was quickly evident that I had joined a class of superstars, whose achievements at Horace Mann were merely the prelude to adult distinction: the serious newspaper editor serving his apprenticeship for a Pulitzer Prize; the flamboyant class president who won acclaim as an art curator and icon of pop culture; the wry intellectual who became a *New Yorker* writer; two talented artists, one an accomplished sculptor and the other a whimsical cartoonist; to say nothing of those honored as "leaders of leaders," who have carved out successful careers in law and medicine.

Even our endless disagreements about the respective merits of Duke Snider, Mickey Mantle, and Willie Mays did not detract from the high seriousness of our common endeavor. (Here, after all, was Talmudic exegesis with an adolescent American accent.) We came to Horace Mann to absorb an intellectual tradition that we respected, the more so since it was not yet ours. It seemed only natural that Christians should teach Jews, for they surely knew what we must learn. Our teachers, to their everlasting credit, were neither arrogant nor patronizing, even at their most terrifying. Indeed, they made it possible for us to imagine that we might leave behind the grubby world of wholesale.

Our grandparents had struggled to speak English; our parents did not attend college. We were expected to transcend their limitations, and we did. There we were, in Wednesday morning assemblies, exuberantly singing "Men of Harlech" while joyously affirming someone else's culture. So many nice Jewish boys from New York, proudly identifying with "Saxon spearmen, Saxon bowmen"! Once Judaism was irrelevant, anything was possible. Religion, according to our school newspaper, merely expressed "minor differences of custom" among people otherwise undifferentiated.

To a teenager who had learned at an early age that Judaism was an impediment to the good things in American life, Horace Mann was perfect. How many places were there, after all, for Jewish boys to affirm their identity among other Jews while simultaneously evading it? But the promised transformation was, for me, incomplete. For graduation, we were instructed to wear a dark (blue or gray) suit, which I had not owned since my bar mitzvah. It was too much to expect my parents to buy one for the occasion, so I never asked. Instead, I bore the shame of wearing an unmatched jacket and trousers. Rather forlornly, I hoped that navy blue mixed with charcoal gray would not testify too conspicuously to my inadequacies. I left Horace Mann as I had entered: inadequately dressed.

Even more debilitating was the graduation-day reality that I still was without a college acceptance. Both my preferred schools, chosen because they most resembled Horace Mann, had rejected me.

I failed to accomplish what even my most doltish classmate had already achieved. For someone as precariously perched on the edge of social acceptance as I was, it was a shameful conclusion to three happy boyhood years.

A month later, finally, I was accepted by Oberlin College. Ohio, but for the Cleveland Indians, hardly existed within my conception of the civilized world, whose outermost western edge was Pittsburgh. I felt banished, doomed to wither in a barren wilderness while my Horace Mann classmates savored the milk and honey of their promised land, triangulated by Cambridge, New Haven and Princeton. I quickly sensed that Oberlin and I were hopelessly mismatched. Its motto, "Learning and Labor," was a throwback to its wholesome rural origins, when students had worked in the fields to earn tuition and strengthen their character. Arriving from New York, sweltering in the late summer heat, I entered a time warp of prairie wholesomeness.

Oberlin, located in what resembled a New England town transplanted to the Western Reserve, was justifiably proud of its history. The first coeducational college, it had once served as a station along the underground railroad from slavery to freedom. But time had stopped in Oberlin not too long after the Wellington slave rescue of 1853, an integral chapter of its historical lore. When I arrived, exactly a century later, I was anything but sophisticated, but I had been to Greenwich Village, eaten in Chinese restaurants, and celebrated the New Year in Times Square. I was accustomed to conversations spiced with irony and wit. Oberlin was all cheery smiles and Gibson's Bakery donuts—wholesome yet indigestible. To my incredulity, I met classmates who actually imagined that they had gone "east" to college.

Oberlin made its most enduring impression at our first Sunday lunch. We stood behind our chairs, forewarned to wait for Mrs. Parker, the "housemother" whose sour visage was a constant reminder to her resident girls to behave themselves, to be seated. Then, spontaneously, everyone (but me) burst into the doxology, ending with fervent praise for "Father, Son and Holy Ghost." Certain that I was back in St. Patrick's Cathedral (I could not yet distinguish between Roman Catholic solemnity and Protestant enthusiasm), I had barely recovered when platters of baked ham appeared before us. I knew little about *kashrut*, but I gagged at the prospect of pig meat. The aftertaste of that Sunday lunch stayed with me for four years.

Even in the mid-1950s, Oberlin was a curious anachronism. Freshman week marked my closest encounter in fifteen years with nursery school. Hayrides, song fests, and games immersed us in a wholesome world of pre-adolescence, which even in my state of arrested maturation seemed silly. Oberlin was a dry town, permitting only 3.2 percent "near-beer" to be sold, and only in a seedy bar next to the solitary local movie theatre. Students were not allowed to bring cars to campus, which was just as well since neither nearby Elyria (which it took me months to pronounce correctly), nor distant Cleveland, was especially enticing. And the next oasis to the west was Toledo.

Left to ourselves, we discovered that freshman girls (neither we nor they ever imagined that they should be insulted by calling them "women") had a 10 P.M. curfew, which hardly mattered since there was no place to go. Boys, of course, were excluded from the girls' dormitories, except for the downstairs living and dining rooms. Rules were strictly enforced at the front door by vigilant housemothers whose formative experiences in the Women's Christian Temperance Union half a century earlier made them formidable adversaries. The only time I ever saw Mrs. Parker smile (and then only grimly) was at the lighting of the dormitory Christmas tree.

Oberlin was disconcerting. Among my high-school friends, language was razor-sharp, double entendres were commonplace, and we bantered incessantly. In Ohio, as far as I could tell, everyone smiled sincerely, thought wholesome thoughts, spoke softly, and never got angry. In what must have been a desperate effort to locate my cultural roots, I attended a Hillel gathering. It was the first time that I ever had to search for other Jews. Sooner or later, I managed to locate a coterie of Jewish friends, all of us bound by our firm determination never to acknowledge that Judaism actually linked us to each other. Our silent code of Jewish self-denial sufficed.

I never for a moment imagined that I belonged in Oberlin. Every year, except during the early fall before the chill of local provincialism set in, or late in the spring when romance predictably bloomed, I always wondered why I was there. During vacations, I returned eagerly to New York, to my Horace Mann friends and, with them, to Greenwich Village coffeehouses, Off-Broadway theatre, Madison Square Garden, and Jones Beach. I envied their exploits and their suffering in Harvard Square and Hanover, but I dutifully completed my four-year sentence, feeling punished for unknown transgressions.

There were occasional moments of satisfaction, and even inspiration. A handful of demanding professors emboldened me to imagine, although I could not yet articulate it, that academe might be an alternative to the jewelry business. During my final year, a young Negro minister named Martin Luther King, Jr., came to speak at Oberlin. The Montgomery bus boycott was then several months along, and rapidly gaining national attention. King, not yet thirty, was its leader. I had read about him, but I was hardly prepared for his passion or for the biblical cadences that echoed through Finney Chapel when he spoke.

Touched by his power and eloquence, I returned to hear him speak again that afternoon, in a local church. During nearly four undergraduate years, it had never occurred to me that black people actually lived in the town of Oberlin; except for a sprinkling of undergraduates, none had ever been visible. Yet there they suddenly were, packed into the local Methodist church, rocking to King's inspirational rhythms, responding with their voices and their bodies to his impassioned cry for racial equality and social justice. Appropriately, as a member of the Silent Generation, I listened silently.

But I remained sufficiently inspired, six months later, to visit his church in Montgomery. A friend and I, the only whites that Sunday morning at the Dexter Avenue Baptist Church, were invited to King's study after the service. There, he fondly recalled his Oberlin visit and graciously expressed his appreciation for our gesture of reciprocity. Afterward, we stood outside with him, absorbing hostile stares from passing whites. But my Montgomery trip defined my limits of permissible political activism.

Throughout my Oberlin years, my father and I engaged in a continuing tug of war over my future. What use was college, he wondered, if it did not direct me to his diamond business. To mollify him temporarily, I became an economics major. A more unlikely choice, this side of physics, I could hardly imagine. I had never answered even a single time/motion problem correctly in two years of high-school algebra, and I was hopelessly confused among the curves and graphs of my economics text. But I grimly persisted through courses in accounting and money and banking until, in desperation, I finally declared my independence.

I wanted to study history, probably because it offered a refuge from my stressful present. For obscure reasons, perhaps related to my fondness as a Jew for underdogs and lost causes, I was fixated on the Civil War. In high school, I had eagerly ransacked second-hand bookstores for war memoirs; once I even accompanied my father on a business trip to Richmond so that I could explore the Virginia battlefields where Stonewall Jackson and Jeb Stuart became legends.

As a college freshman, I wrote my first research paper about General George McClellan, an early commander of the Union armies. His paralysis of will on the eve of battle may have reminded me of my own recurrent bouts of indecision. That assignment gave me privileged access to the library stacks. There, I discovered an exhilarating mixture of intellectual excitement and solitary tranquility. I located McClellan's memoirs, critically annotated with handwritten insertions by a general under his command, Jacob D. Cox, whose library had been donated to Oberlin. Their fascinating historical dialogue instantly brought the past to life for me.

As captivated as I was by history, majoring in it seemed far too indulgent—especially to my father. What good was it? What could I do with it? Unable to answer his questions, I chose political science as a tolerable path toward a useful career: law. (Since my father's business partner had once earned his law degree in night school, law did not automatically disqualify me, as did history, from a life devoted to selling diamonds.) I could at least deflect my father, even if I could not yet defeat him. As a modest reward, I even discovered a measure of fascination in my constitutional law course, taught by a frosty curmudgeon whose full three names contained only five syllables. To this day, Percy Thomas Fenn remains the only person I ever met who was forever proud that he had voted for Herbert Hoover in 1932.

I was at a complete loss to decide what would actually follow college. We all were somewhat intimidated into political caution by McCarthyism. (My father's most memorable admonition, issued while urging me never to sign a political petition, was: "Don't get involved.") My constricted sense of possibilities was further narrowed by the military draft, which beckoned the moment that any of us left school. The army, I sensed, was not a good place for Jews. Furthermore, school was where I had always been; and leaving it permanently behind was the closest thing I could then imagine to an unnatural act. My friends, to whom I attributed wisdom far beyond my own, had all decided to become lawyers. Certain that they knew what was best, I followed them to law school.

If my father anticipated my legal training as preparation for life on West 47th Street, I fantasized a career as an American Civil Liberties Union litigator, arguing First Amendment cases before the Supreme Court. (The irony of my identification with social outcasts, as long as they were not Jewish, was not yet apparent to me.) It took about a week of slogging through the legal trenches, otherwise known as contracts and civil procedure, before I realized that I had made a horrendous mistake. Columbia Law School not only was located on the same subway line as Wall Street; it was on the same career line. If partnership in the Ide Jewelry Company filled me with dread, the prospect of a life indentured to corporate clients evoked sheer terror.

After one semester of legal torture (alleviated only by the random good fortune that I was never called on in class), I went to sleep, literally, for the better part of three months. I roused myself for nothing more demanding than afternoon movies, the most decadent act of rebellion I could imagine. When I finally escaped this paralyzing torpor, I summoned the courage to inform my father that I intended to leave law school to study history. He was predictably upset, for my decision irrevocably frustrated his plan for our business partnership. I could not reassure him about my future, since I had absolutely no idea what a doctorate might entail other than prolonged confinement to school, which was all the incentive I needed. I left the law with a perfect record as a litigator, enjoying a moot court verdict from a sitting municipal court judge who assured me that a fine legal career awaited me.

Fortified by an impulsive purchase of Charles and Mary Beard's massive *History of American Civilization* (not one page of which I ever read), I became a graduate student. In truth, graduate school was not, at first, much of an improvement over law school. My new preoccupation with dreary historiographical debates about the causes of the American revolution or the sources of Jacksonian democracy was not significantly more inspiring than the rule against perpetuities. But I had exhausted my options.

I did, however, finally take an American history course that not only reached the twentieth century but actually began there. Studying Puritans or abolitionists appealed to my latent sympathies for fanatics, but there was something especially compelling about the only period of American history that coincided with the presence of my own family in the United States. To be sure, Jews never were mentioned in any lecture, nor did they appear on any reading list. But I stumbled upon Samuel Lubell's *The Future of American Politics*, which analyzed the contribution of ethnic minorities to the Roosevelt electoral upheaval of 1936 (the year of my birth). It touched a hidden nerve of interest.

Excited, I wrote to my Oberlin mentor. I valued his steadfast encouragement. I had consulted him when my father and I battled over my decision to leave law school, and indeed, his confidence in my abilities vastly exceeded my own. He had reassured me that my decision to become a historian was not an automatic confession of failure, despite the lingering doubts that paternal disapproval conferred. I explained to him that I planned to write my master's degree thesis on the political behavior of American Jews during the Depression, a subject already much better known to me than I imagined.

He replied, with delicacy, that I should be careful lest my choice of subject label me in a way that might subsequently prove disadvantageous when I looked for a teaching position. (As a lapsed Jew whose scholarly specialty was Negro history, he had every reason to make the point.) When I broached my idea to my Columbia adviser, whose scholarship had ground to a halt with his doctoral thesis twenty years earlier, he puffed his pipe contemplatively before quizzing me about my mastery of foreign languages. Forewarned that "Jewish" was "foreign," I wrote instead about Fiorello LaGuardia, the colorful half-Jewish mayor of New Deal New York, whose radio recitations of the Sunday comic strips lingered as a fond childhood memory.

As a graduate student I rarely left the past or the library. But there were compensations. My undergraduate delight in uncovering General McClellan's foibles was replicated in researching my first doctoral seminar paper. I discovered that some distinguished turn-of-the-century reformers, beneath their lofty liberal rhetoric, had been rather conventional racists. After converting the paper into my first published article, I realized that I had finally done work that I truly enjoyed. With a token payment from the journal, even my father was pleased.

Flushed by success, I was sufficiently emboldened to accept a blind date with a Barnard student, an Orthodox Jew. But as I traveled by subway to Washington Heights (known because of its many German Jewish World War II refugees as Frankfurt-on-the-Hudson), I felt dismaying tugs of memory from long-ago visits to my Old World relatives. Her parents' apartment was every bit as dark and gloomy as I had anticipated. Surely her father must be a rabbi, for he precisely fit my preconceived image: pale, gray-bearded, and remote.

As I waited for his daughter, his prolonged silence (he was, I imagined, praying for me to leave) heightened my nervous apprehension. In the end, she was worth waiting for: strikingly attractive in a bright, tight dress, she broke through her drab surroundings like a dazzling rainbow. She knew it—and so, of course, did her father. Even more unsettled, I spent most of the evening trying to reconcile the evident disparity between Orthodox solemnity and feminine glamour. Failing, I never called her again.

My preference, by far, was for a companion in Jewish ambivalence. I discovered another Barnard student, even more attractive and culturally refined; every bit as comfortable in the Metropolitan Museum as I was in Madison Square Garden. Traveling by subway to her Brooklyn home, I felt slightly trapped by the geographical reminder of my own family heritage of Jewish discomfort. But, among other shared pleasures, we collaborated in relentlessly challenging her parents, whose engaged Judaism and passionate Zionism violated our shared conception of cultural dignity. Our wedding, presided over by her family rabbi in an elegant Central Park South hotel chosen by my parents, precisely reflected our Jewish yearning for American acceptance.

Midway through graduate school, in a fortuitous twist of fate, I was invited to write the biography of Joseph M. Proskauer, a prominent elderly New York lawyer. The ironies were almost comical. A law-school dropout, I would now dedicate myself to analyzing the career of an extremely successful corporate lawyer, a man whose political allegiance to Al Smith had assured him a seat on the Supreme Court, but for Herbert Hoover's election in 1928. A fervent New Dealer, I would keep the company of a man whose contempt for F.D.R. had driven him to vote for every Republican presidential candidate beginning with Alf Landon in 1936. A Jewish drop-out, I would be writing about a prominent figure in American Jewish politics during the 1940s, an outspoken anti-Zionist who had anticipated a Jewish state as an unmitigated calamity for American Jews.

The offer from Proskauer's law firm, both flattering and financially alluring, also seemed so diabolically appropriate that I could hardly decline. But I quickly discovered the depths of my folly. There I was, commuting every morning to my law office. There I sat all day, poring endlessly through appellate case files, trucked by the cartload from warehouse storage. They dealt with subjects far less interesting than anything that had bored me during my dreariest days as a law student. When, in desperation, I searched for some interesting correspondence about Democratic politics that might at least keep me awake, I learned that it had all been consumed by fire, or lost in transit, or destroyed by rodents years before. Even the thick files of Jewish materials that sparked my curiosity had been carefully pruned, the better to conceal the depths of Proskauer's prolonged antipathy to the Zionist cause.

As a hired gun, I learned that I was expected to be as deferential toward "the Judge," as everyone in the firm addressed Proskauer, as were the young associates and aging partners who nearly genuflected in his presence. I did what little I could to protect my integrity. I never wore a tie, and I returned from my summer vacation sporting a mustache that was a violation of corporate legal norms. When the office manager rebuked me for my appearance and suggested that I might be offending clients, I offered to shave my mustache if the Judge removed his. By then, our patience with each other was exhausted. Midway through the year we negotiated my release.

After that experience, graduate school was less onerous. Left alone to read and write, I navigated my way toward my doctorate, past inscrutable professors and around interminable requirements. When an excerpt from my dissertation won a professional prize, my decision to become a historian seemed vindicated. But once it finally came time to find a teaching position, I managed to assure myself even more exquisite misery than a Jewish law firm had provided. I joined the faculty of Brandeis University.

The idea of a Jewish university had floated around for decades, only to be repeatedly sabotaged by wealthy German Jews (who could easily have funded such a school but preferred to identify with Harvard). Finally launched in 1948, the university remained the institutional shadow of Abram Sachar, its founder and diabolical financial wizard. Sachar had intuitively grasped the insecurities and yearnings of second-generation Jewish businessmen, who responded enthusiastically to his educational sales pitch. These merchants and entrepreneurs, whose parents had been peddlers in Eastern Europe, eagerly depleted their private fortunes to create the first non-sectarian Jewish university in the United States.

Brandeis was known among cynics as Sachar's own edifice complex. The monotonously uniform brick and glass buildings were huddled so closely together that, as one waggish colleague observed, they needed only clotheslines strung between them to faithfully replicate the Lower East Side. The names of donors were everywhere: on buildings, laboratories, classrooms, alcoves, and even—in one of Sachar's cleverest schemes—on subdivisions of the air space above its Waltham campus.

The university's proudest architectural boast, the three chapels that were clustered in a remote corner of the campus, symbolized its split vision. It was difficult to imagine any university, other than one nondenominationally Jewish, so committed to such a conspicuous architectural display of its tolerant ecumenicism—at a time when the library still had hardly any books.

Sachar, who quite literally had created the silk purse of a modern university out of the sow's ear of a decrepit veterinary school, still reigned supreme when I arrived in the mid-1960s. Indeed, he exercised power in a fashion that would have made any divine-right monarch quiver with envy. At Brandeis, he was the undisputed king of the Jews. Once, I had the temerity to write a mildly critical letter to the editor of a university magazine about the frustrating inadequacies of the library. I was promptly admonished—by Sachar himself, who evidently had informants everywhere—that it would be in the best interests of my career to demonstrate appreciation for institutional virtues. When I showed the letter to an esteemed senior colleague who was renowned for his vigorous defense of freedom of speech, he advised me to apologize immediately and, if possible, abjectly.

Brandeis was Jewish bedlam. Its schizophrenic mission—to become a Jewish Harvard—converted it into a repository of Jewish intellectual and cultural angst. I was fascinated and repelled both by the precociousness of students and by the arrogance of colleagues. I quickly learned that outrageous verbal pyrotechnics, whether in class or in faculty debates, were always rewarded. For a historian of modern America, Brandeis was ideal: the perfect vantage point for witnessing, in microcosm, the unfolding of all the bizarre excesses of the 1960s.

Its oddly juxtaposed Jewish features made Brandeis simultaneously appealing and appalling. All the Jewish holidays were observed, and I even discovered one, Shmini Atzeret, whose existence was entirely unknown to me. However, department meetings were routinely scheduled for Saturday mornings, and my Jewish colleagues knew far less Yiddish than John Roche, the only Irish Catholic among us.

Nothing more vividly characterized Brandeis, at the time, than the relentless striving of its *arriviste* academics. Every bit as entrepreneurial as our university benefactors, they had learned that careers and books, like stock options, were products to be hustled in the academic marketplace. And hustle they did: book contracts were dangled everywhere; ideas for ever-newer texts and multi-volume series sprouted like mushrooms after a summer rain.

As junior faculty, we quickly learned that appointments and promotions followed the same principles of fickle avarice that guided Wall Street speculators. Colleagues came and went through the revolving doors of ambition and reputation, according to their momentary street value. Depending upon forecasts in the professional journals, the department might suddenly become bullish on social or comparative history. Once the tenured bears growled, it was time for the downgraded medievalist or German historian to move elsewhere.

Striving to become a Jewish Harvard exacted the heaviest toll on my colleagues who were, after all, only at Brandeis. One of them, palpably eager to return to the scene of his graduate-student glory, hyperventilated at the merest mention of Harvard. Another, our chameleon, uncannily aligned himself with the vote of the tenured majority on every issue, no matter how trivial. Yet another was seen each week balancing a new pile of library books on his shoulder, the better to display his voracious appetite for the most obscure new monographs in the most recondite fields. Our newest member, spirited from the Ivy League with lavish promises of empire, spent two years prowling through the halls, plotting his next power grab. Had I been less insecure, I might have tried harder to understand what made these academic Sammys run, or why I so readily chased after them.

In this deranged setting, I chose my own personal mentor despite his reputation for brusque crassness. I was quite prepared to accept small humiliations (like fetching his sandwiches) in return for protection from my colleagues. The arrangement served us both. It reassured me and may have compensated him for his own days of academic peonage. In graduate school, he recounted, his imperious mentor had dispatched him across Broadway with bundles of dirty laundry. My secret consolation, highly prized, was the chance discovery of a cache of his letters in the Library of Congress, written not long after his appointment to the Brandeis faculty. His own debilitating insecurities as a young instructor had plunged him into depths of academic servility, especially toward President Sachar. After I shared my findings with other junior colleagues, we all felt slightly less humiliated by his arrogance.

As a non-sectarian Jewish university, Brandeis featured its own distinctive mix of tormented European refugees, debonair Marxists, and pompous poets who enlivened faculty meetings with their histrionics. Our department was less fortunate: collegial relations were so strained that we even convened a constitutional convention to draft rules of civilized behavior (none of which could we summon a majority to ratify). During my second year, I was actually elected chairman of the graduate program (for a term that lasted twenty-four hours) because the two more obvious candidates could not tolerate each other's company. It hardly mattered: our unvarying agenda was to assess the prospect of enticing some rising academic star to join us or to decide how best to coax unwary but talented graduate students into our lair.

In the baseball metaphors that still made the most sense to me, I came to understand Brandeis as the academic triple-A league. Aspiring stars passed briefly through on their way to Yale or Berkeley. Veterans, their successes mostly behind them, clung to their tenured sinecures. Some were not wanted elsewhere; others clearly enjoyed the opportunity to merchandise their wares in a congenial marketplace; occasionally, someone actually managed to carve out a private space for good work amid the zaniness, before departing for more civilized surroundings.

By the late '60s, however, increasingly volatile and narcissistic students (whose extra-curricular activities included seizing one Brandeis building and torching another) had all but transformed quiet contemplation into a subversive activity. Those students were, in their own way, quite remarkable; and I never have taught any others with nearly as much intellectual spark. But the Vietnam War frazzled their minds; and as they verbalized or acted out their wildest fantasies of adolescent rebellion, they were quite as maddening as they were engaging. Then, too, I envied their rebellious freedom. It far exceeded anything I had ever permitted myself to imagine when I was their age.

Although its Jewish assertions and evasions were altogether familiar, Brandeis reminded me too much of the vulgar commercialism of West 47th Street, which I had hoped to avoid in academe. That my boyhood New England fantasy should actually be realized, near Boston if not in the Berkshires, was remarkable enough. That it was at Brandeis, rather than Williams or Amherst, seemed altogether appropriate retribution for my prolonged Jewish ambivalence.

With my first children born and my first book published, living in the first house that anyone in my immediate family had ever owned (as remote from the "Jewish" suburbs of Brookline and Newton as possible), I settled serenely upon the plateau of middle age when I was barely past thirty. I was completely comfortable with my life as a non-Jewish Jew. My New Deal liberalism was still intact. I had even managed to accumulate sufficient self-confidence to withstand the abrupt shock of tenure denial. Grateful for my freedom, even if I wished that I had initiated it, I prepared to trade the Jewish hypermania of Brandeis for the female civility of Wellesley College.

A LIFE OF ACADEMIC TRANQUILITY BECKONED ENTICINGLY. For three months I was calmed by Wellesley serenity. Then I met a colleague who was leaving for Israel to participate in a seminar for Jewish professors. I had never visited the Jewish state nor thought much about it. The Proskauer firm had promised a trip to Israel to interview Ben-Gurion and other luminaries who might certify the Judge's importance, but once our relations soured it never was mentioned again. My parents went once for a reunion with my father's family, but they spoke only of the food (unpalatable) and the heat (unbearable). Even the Six Day War had all but passed me by, so distracted was I with my three-week-old daughter. Israel was remote and I was indifferent.

But the prospect of a free trip was irresistible. And, surely, the destination was not irrelevant. The seminar, sponsored by the American Jewish Committee, was designed to rouse slumbering scholars from their Jewish self-denial, the better to combat the poisonous New Left anti-Zionism that had begun to contaminate American campus life. After a mortifying interview during which the depth of my Jewish confusion was evident to all, I realized that I was a perfect candidate. So, to its chagrin, did the Committee, which dutifully invited me to participate. I cherished the irony, for this was the very organization that Proskauer had guided to its resolutely anti-Zionist position before the birth of the Jewish state. Now it would send me to Israel.

I did not anticipate how quickly or abruptly I would confront history, memory, and myself. Our flight to Tel Aviv stopped briefly in Frankfurt. Touching down in a dense fog, we taxied endlessly to a remote corner of the airport. Suddenly the plane was surrounded—I hallucinated—by heavily armed Nazi soldiers. Enclosed in fog and fatigue, I finally realized that the jack-booted Germans were assigned to protect us against the hijacking terror for which Palestinians had already become notorious.

I had been to Germany once before in 1959. I had not wanted to go, nor could I stay away. I was anxious throughout my visit. Nearly fifteen years after World War II had ended, Munich was still a bombed out shell of a city. Driven by impulses I could neither explain nor repress, I searched relentlessly for the only remaining synogogue in the entire city. But I could not speak German, and the unintelligible guttural answers I received to my questions set me even more on edge. Finally, in a bizarre moment of frustration, I drew the Star of David on a piece of paper and showed it to the customers in a butcher shop in the old Jewish neighborhood. While they stared impassively, the butcher pointed me toward the synagogue. I never found it.

I did make a pilgrimage to Dachau. The suburban train from Munich was filled with men just the right age to have herded Jews into cattle cars and gas chambers. At the edge of town, I searched for the camp site, not yet a manicured shrine along the Holocaust tourist trail. Inside the perimeter of a United States army base, a sergeant, visibly puzzled by my determination and my destination, directed me down the road to a barbed-wire enclosure. Rotting watchtowers guarded vacant barracks. It was hauntingly empty.

Dachau, I knew, was not a Nazi extermination camp. But it had its own gas chamber, which I entered to stare at the overhead nozzles. I found a row of ovens, blackened with the ashes of Jews. Nearby, huge mounds marked mass graves. I was numb, unable to speak, scream, or cry. I did not think to recite *kaddish*, because I did not know how. These were the buried memories that suddenly resurfaced in the dim morning fog of Frankfurt, when German soldiers surrounded my plane to protect me from the newest enemies of the Jews.

Late that night in Jerusalem, too exhilarated to sleep, I walked to the Old City. Inside the Jaffa Gate, I carefully followed a Hasidic Jew, wearing clothes as black as the night. He led me, as I instinctively knew he would, through darkened alleys to the narrow passage that brought me to the steps leading down to the Western Wall. Brightly lit, stark and vast, the Wall dwarfed the pious men who had gathered there in prayer. I hesitated to approach, but I was too mesmerized to retreat. My gaze was riveted on the massive Herodion stones that until that moment I had never imagined might be my home address as a Jew.

For two weeks I was bombarded by acutely conflicted feelings of attraction and resistance. My delicate internal balance of Jewish ambivalence was suddenly precarious. Judaism had always been a source of uneasy disaffection. When it evoked the foreign accents of my European relatives or recalled the evasions of my parents, I wanted nothing to do with it. Too Jewish to feel comfortably American, I was too American to be comfortably Jewish.

In Israel, these disconnected fragments of my own Jewish confusion were combustible. They suddenly burst into the flame of impassioned encounters with our seminar leader, Yehuda Rosenman. Yehuda instantly emerged as my newest and most formidable adversary in an endless line of surrogate fathers with whom I had continuously fought out the unresolved issues of my childhood. I simultaneously loved and hated all of them—coaches, teachers, mentors, public figures alike—in various proportions and for different reasons. But Yehuda was the first strongly identified Jew among them, so he engaged my passions as none of his predecessors had.

Yehuda had grown up in pre-war Poland in a circle of committed Zionists that included the family of Menachem Begin. Fleeing the Nazis, he came to the United States, where he worked for various Jewish social service agencies. At the American Jewish Committee (which, of course, I secretly held against him), he was an anomaly. An ebullient and charming man, fluent in Hebrew and Yiddish, he was passionate about Israel. Yet he worked for a bureaucracy dominated by assimilated, buttoned-down philanthropists who had yet to wean themselves (or the Committee) from their own nagging trepidation about being "too Jewish" for American comfort.

Yehuda flourished in Israel, where he struggled with extravagant hope for the Jewish souls of the disaffected academics who came his way every year. I knew that he wanted us to recognize Israel as a miraculous incarnation of Jewish historical imperatives, but he asked only that we apply to the Jewish state a measure of the critical intelligence for which we, as diaspora intellectuals, were renowned. Then, we might help to counter the slanderous assaults against Israel that pervaded normal academic discourse. For Jews like us, that was asking a lot.

Many Israelis forced me to confront the core principle of my American Jewish faith: the facile equation of Judaism with liberalism. One Orthodox intellectual (a Jewish oxymoron, I believed) insisted that the Jewish religious tradition still posed the most urgent questions for modern Jews, and—unlike Western liberalism—might even answer them. A Russian film director, recently arrived from Kiev, candidly explained why his favorite Israeli was not Golda Meir or Moshe Dayan, but Rabbi Meir Kahane. An army officer, with uncommon sensitivity to the psychic toll exacted from Israelis by perpetual military preparedness, rejected our glib Vietnam analogies. He thoroughly embarrassed a panel of Israeli leftist intellectuals, who airily dismissed any notion of "secure borders" or "biblical heritage" as rhetorical nonsense. Little children in Jerusalem's ultra-Orthodox neighborhood of Mea Shearim, a living Polish shtetl, scurried from our path in a graphic display of their discomfort with Jewish intruders from modernity.

Confused but riveted, I felt an irrepressible yearning to come back to Jerusalem, indeed to live there. Instead, I returned to the musty depths of the Harvard Law School library to complete my research for a history of the American legal profession, whose blandishments I had once spurned. I had begun to discover irrefutable evidence of half a century of rampant and persistent anti-Semitism in law schools, law firms, and bar associations. Now I seized on the material anew, for the historical documents forced me to confront some deeply tangled threads of autobiography and Jewish history.

Still a "good liberal," I was outraged to discover the perversions of equality and justice that had infiltrated the loftiest realms of the legal profession. Rather more slowly, I realized that anti-Semitism deeply offended me as a Jew. During my search for the proper scholarly language to express the intensity of my feelings, I received a telephone inquiry from Israel. Would I consider a Fulbright professorship at Tel Aviv University? I weighed the invitation for the duration of a heartbeat, and accepted.

It was not long before my enthusiasm was severely tested. During that spring of 1974, Palestinian terrorists went on a rampage. Crossing the Lebanese border, they burst into an apartment building in the northern Israeli town of Kiryat Shemona, where I had visited a year earlier. There, in the school building where we had conferred with municipal officials, the PLO indiscriminately murdered eighteen Israelis, including women and children, before they were killed. A month later, another band of Palestinian terrorists seized a school in nearby Ma'alot, where they took more than one hundred children hostage. Twenty children died when Israeli soldiers assaulted the building. The following month, in Nahariya (where I had once strolled along the tree-lined canal that bisects this peaceful resort), yet another terrorist attack claimed the lives of a mother and her two young children.

Friends reassured me that I was not expected to share such risks, nor impose them on Jeff and Pammy, my young children. American discretion, they implied, might be the better part of Jewish valor. By then, however, six years of incessant public turmoil, from the Tet offensive through the King and Kennedy assassinations to Watergate, had all but unraveled my identification with the United States. Feeling like a man without a country, I was ready to become a wandering Jew in Israel.

Israel had changed dramatically since my previous visit. In 1972, the euphoria after the Six Day War was still palpable. By 1974, when I returned, the nation, devastated by the Yom Kippur War, was in shock. Preoccupied with such mundane activities as opening a bank account, enrolling children in school, and determining the contents of jars and cans from indecipherable Hebrew labels, I hardly noticed. But the fragility of Israeli public life and the tight interlacing of public events and private moods was inescapable. Accustomed to retreating from the public affairs of my own country, I was totally unprepared for the unsettling experience of national identification.

One hot September afternoon, we roamed the Old City walls and explored new archeological excavations outside the Dung Gate.

Dusty and sweaty, we walked back along Ramban Street, normally bustling with noisy traffic in the late afternoon. Now it was strangely silent. Every store was closed. Nothing moved. I was oblivious, until that moment, to the imminence of Yom Kippur and to the meaning of its observance in a Jewish state. In my family, even this holiest day in the Jewish calendar usually passed without recognition. Suddenly, in Jerusalem, I was humiliated by my indifference.

Silently climbing four flights of stairs to our apartment, I may even have prayed that none of our neighbors would see us. We ate cautiously, lest any sound of kitchen noises bear witness to our violation of this day of fasting. The next morning, forsaking synagogue services, we walked to the nearby Valley of the Cross, beneath the Israel Museum. Jerusalem, immersed in silent stillness, had disappeared inside itself. In an entire hour, along one of the busiest boulevards in the city, only a military jeep and an ambulance passed by. A mute spectator, I remained isolated, outside the day.

The first anniversary of the outbreak of the Yom Kippur War also caught me by surprise. Late one morning, sirens wailed their eerie cadences through a suddenly hushed city. When I stepped outside to our balcony, overlooking one of the noisiest intersections in residential Jerusalem, every vehicle appeared to have been abandoned in place. People were frozen. Below me, a man stood by his car in the middle of the street, his head bowed. Watching him, I felt transformed from a spectator to a mourner in our shared vigil.

Those early months in Israel were difficult, even painful. None of my fantasies of identification were fulfilled. Isolated by language and culture, encased in my Jewish ignorance, buffeted by the abrasiveness of daily life in an unfamiliar place, I took refuge in endless walks. I criss-crossed the mosaic of Jerusalem neighborhoods, secular and religious, Arab and Israeli, Sephardi and Ashkenazi. Struggling to make Jerusalem mine, I searched endlessly for clues to Jewish mysteries that I could not yet even identify.

One November morning, on my weekly commute to Tel Aviv, the staccato beeps of the *sherut* radio brought the mandatory hush for the hourly news broadcast. A palpable shudder rippled through the other passengers. An anguished discussion consumed the rest of our ride. I caught the name of a place, Beit Shean, but nothing more until I reached the university. There, Rafi, one of my students (and best teachers), located it for me on an improvised map. Yet another terrorist raid, this one from Jordan, had killed four Israelis and injured dozens of others.

Just the week before, Yasir Arafat had made his notorious appearance before the United Nations, brandishing a pistol on his hip, to proclaim that Zionism was "imperialistic, colonialist, racist." In place of Israel, he demanded "a democratic Palestine." The obsequious fawning of the West, still eager to appease those who shed innocent Jewish blood, infuriated Israelis. So did Western media coverage of the Beit Shean massacre. More American editorial invective was heaped upon the Sephardic Jews who had mutilated the bodies of the dead terrorists than upon the Arabs who had murdered living Jews.

For months, I maintained my status as an unimplicated outsider. Then, at sunrise on the day before Chanukah vacation, my family boarded a bus in Jerusalem for a camping trip in Sinai. I was sufficiently awake to notice among our fellow travelers half a dozen American students from a Jerusalem yeshiva. Their scraggly beards, *kippot*, and dangling *tzitzit* boldly proclaimed their Orthodoxy. I would more readily have welcomed Bedouin, or even Eskimos. The prospect of spending a week with yeshiva students generated visceral discomfort that did not recede until, many hours later, we sped along the breathtakingly beautiful Sinai coast toward Dahab.

We finally bounced to a halt in total desert darkness. As duffel and sleeping bags cascaded down from the roof of the bus, we groped for our belongings, staked out campsites, and searched for prepackaged manna to feed the children. But the yeshiva boys had other priorities. While we scurried about frenetically, they unpacked a menorah and lit the first candles of Chanukah. Reciting the blessings, they instantly drew us together. In this vast wilderness of ancient revelation, we sang *Ma-oz Tsur* (which I had not heard since Hebrew school). I was suddenly gripped with deep sorrow for my own years of desert wandering. Nothing during our week of assorted Sinai adventures had as much impact as those tiny pinpoints of flickering light and the childhood memory of a Jewish song.

We returned to Jerusalem with barely enough time to shower, eat, and race to the Western Wall for the lighting of the final Chanukah candles. The plaza in front of the Wall was packed, the festive mood contrasting sharply with the brooding solemnity that normally hovered over the layered courses of ancient stones. We even stumbled happily upon Gedaliah and Hershel, the two yeshiva boys from our Sinai expedition who had managed to entertain the children when parental patience was exhausted.

As we strained to hear the rabbi complete his blessings, a loud whoosh, followed by a spreading orange glow, ignited a row of nine huge oil vats high above us. Simultaneously, a thousand Jews sang together. That night at the Western Wall, I participated unselfconsciously in a ritual of Jewish ceremonial observance. For the first time.

Back in our apartment, buried among the bills and newspapers that had accumulated in our absence, was a letter of concern from an American friend. She had kept her silence during the fall, despite the terrorist attacks, Arafat's triumphal appearance at the U.N., and the Rabat Conference where Arab states had pledged their unrelenting military and economic hostility to "the Zionist enemy." Now, following a military alert in Syria, there were ominous rumblings of renewed conflict on Israel's northern border. Unable to quell her anxiety, she inquired about our contingency plans for leaving Israel if war erupted.

Just back from the Western Wall, in the flush of Sinai, I could not comprehend her apprehension. I began to enumerate all the procedural impediments to our departure if war began: How would we obtain money or tickets, or even reach the airport? Would there be civilian flights? But, I quickly realized, it was not a matter of tickets or taxis. Rather, it was an issue of identification and attachment.

I was a Jew, in Israel. Could I possibly say to our few Israeli friends, but especially to myself, that the Jewish state was not safe for me? Would I leave, abandoning Israelis to their Jewish fate? I might still have doubts about those Israelis who referred to the

"Jewish nation," and I might question my inclusion in it as an American Jew. Certainly I was still puzzled whenever Israelis asked if I planned to live permanently in Israel. Why should I? Yet I felt attachments too powerful to deny. As delightful as a Greek island holiday sounded, I knew that I must remain in Jerusalem.

Despite my decision, my internal compass still pointed more toward American estrangement than Jewish identification. Israel tapped my disaffection with the United States; one that had been growing since my final flush of boyhood patriotism at the end of World War II. My choice of an academic career had been designed to elude a culture of material acquisitiveness. My friends were disaffected Jewish intellectuals, all of us congenitally unable to commit ourselves to anything but ironic detachment from our own society. My career as a professional historian provided a retreat to the past, where I could quietly remain oblivious to daily reality.

But Israel confirmed how truly American I was. Where else would anyone describe me as "Anglo-Saxon"? My instinct, whenever I was searched at the entrances to Israeli museums, libraries, or supermarkets, was to cite the Fourth Amendment. I was a middle-class suburban academic, whose center of the universe was Harvard Square. I expected bookstores and cinemas to be open and buses to run for my convenience, not to close for the Jewish Sabbath.

In Israel, even my signals to my children had become hopelessly confused. Why must their Jerusalem school be guarded by parents with guns? Why must they be warned not to pick up anything from the ground, no matter how tempting? One day my young son and I walked along Ramban Street, licking ice-cream cones. We spotted a letter on the sidewalk, next to a mailbox. Surely it had fallen accidentally. Why not pick it up and mail it? Because school posters warned that discarded candy boxes, coins, buttons—and letters—all could be used by terrorists to conceal bombs. We debated: should we (be Americans), or should we not? We moved on.

In my Tel Aviv class, certain American reflexes still predominated. I offered a course I had taught at Wellesley, entitled "The American Promised Land." I had designed it during the late '60s, with thinly concealed irony that my American students readily detected and appreciated. During the Nixon administration, in the years between Kent State and Watergate, who could possibly take American "promise" seriously? Israelis still did. They found nothing incongruous in an American professor teaching about the American promised land in the promised Jewish homeland. The tenacity of their attachment to the American dream astonished me, just as my cynicism astounded them.

Rafi, my favorite student, delighted in showing me old Tel Aviv, his Tel Aviv, far from the glitz of the beachfront hotels that swarmed with American tourists. Occasionally, he came to Jerusalem to take me to a neighborhood that had a story he wanted to share. But I never asked him to retell his story of the morning of June 7, 1967. With a division of Israeli paratroopers, Rafi had raced through the Lion's Gate of the Old City, across the Temple Mount, through the Magreb Gate, and down a narrow flight of steps to the Western Wall, suddenly restored to Jewish sovereignty for the first time in two thousand years.

Rafi, a Kol Israel broadcaster, was on the air, his voice quivering with excitement and choking with tears. "I'm not religious and never have been," he had blurted out, "but this is the Wall and I am touching the stones of the Western Wall!" In Sinai, soldiers had jumped down from their half-tracks to hear Rafi's words, punctuated by the blowing of a *shofar*, then *kaddish*, and finally *Hatikvah*. "He did not talk with the newspaperman's objectivity," a soldier recalled in an interview; "he wasn't articulate, he couldn't even control the recording machine he was carrying. That's why we all felt how history was beating its wings."

Everywhere in Israel during that year, the wings of Jewish history were beating nearby. In Hebron, I felt the palpable hostility of Arabs in the casbah, the old Jewish quarter before the massacres of 1929 drove Jews away. My son Jeff and I explored Kypros, the Herodian fortress overlooking the hills of Moab where the Israelites had crossed the Jordan River into Canaan. In nearby Nauron, we admired the splendid mosaic floor of a recently discovered ancient synagogue. With foolhardy innocence, I drove my family through the heart of Samaria to Shiloh, where the Ark of the Covenant, bearing the stone tablets from Sinai, had rested.

Nothing seared me more than an encounter at Lohamei Hagettaot, a kibbutz founded by Warsaw ghetto survivors. Our visit be-

gan as a classic Israeli misadventure. We appeared at the kibbutz
museum during its advertised open hours, only to discover that it
was closed. I knocked politely, then banged loudly. A janitor
peered out, disappeared, and finally returned to open the museum
for our exclusive benefit. The Ghetto Fighters museum, with its
powerful message of Jewish resistance, instantly confronted me
with all the self-hating Jewish stereotypes from my childhood
about six million Jews shuffling like sheep to the gas chambers.
Emotionally exhausted from the encounter, I fixated upon a display case with a single pair of tiny shoes. From a million Jewish
children who had been my age during the Holocaust, little more
than these shoes remained.

As I stared in pained silence, the janitor reappeared to beckon
us to the office of the museum director, a handsome woman in her
fifties. She brusquely asked some perfunctory questions in thickly
accented English about my background, my reasons for being in
Israel, my response to the exhibits. I mentioned the shoes. Suddenly she erupted, her eyes blazing with fury. I was, she reminded
me, old enough to remember the Holocaust. I might have been
among those children. I was a Jew. How, then, could I justify my
decision not to live in Israel?

Foolishly imagining that I might stem her tirade with a reasoned
response, I tried to explain. I was, after all, American; I had, nonetheless, decided to spend my sabbatical year in Israel; and I did,
certainly, believe in the necessity of a Jewish state. She interrupted:
if I truly cared about Jewish children, how could I raise mine to
live in *galut*? Now I remained silent, knowing that I had no answers to satisfy her. I wondered whether they would, any longer,
satisfy me. Finally she subsided, inscribed a book about the museum, and led us to the exit.

She was, I learned, Tzivia Lubetkin, a legendary member of the
Jewish underground in Poland, and a heroic fighter in the Warsaw
ghetto uprising. With Antek Zuckerman (her husband), who or-
ganized the revolt, and Mordechai Anielewicz, who commanded
the ghetto fighters, she led the Jewish resistance. With the ghetto a
flaming inferno, she finally escaped through the sewers to rejoin
Antek. Only fifteen ghetto survivors still were alive in 1950; seven,
including Antek and Tzivia, were among the founders of the kib-

butz, dedicated to the memory of the ghetto fighters. I never forgot her searing rage, or her questions.

For a year, Jerusalem was my constant companion. Exploring the city, I finally began to encounter myself as a Jew. I frequently retraced my steps to the Western Wall, pulled inexorably back by memories from my first night in Israel. There I would sit, sometimes for hours, watching the Hasidim endlessly form and reform their *minyanim* for prayer. With my beard, I must have seemed a likely recruit, for I was occasionally asked to join, or invited to wrap *t'fillin*. Too embarrassed to display my ignorance, since I did not know what to say or do, I always declined. I wanted to be left alone to observe, not to participate.

On the damp, chilly days for which Jerusalem winters are notorious, I often retreated inside the high vaulted stone chambers adjacent to the Wall, beneath Wilson's Arch. There, in the dim light, I was invariably lulled into dreamy contemplation by the rhythmic murmur of prayers, and by the choreographed rituals of the men who drifted in and out to recite them.

Late one Friday afternoon, I was roused from my repose by a haunting cantorial melody, sharply penetrating even from a distance. Its ecstatic cadences held me enthralled. As the *chazzan*, a bearded old man wrapped in a *tallit*, approached, his voice pierced deeply into my memory. Instantly I was transported back to the Friday evenings of my childhood, when Cantor Gorsky had proclaimed the arrival of the Sabbath through our living-room wall. As voice and memory merged, they reverberated through the caverns of my buried Jewish self. Suddenly I yearned to return to my childhood and relive my life, this time as a Jew.

When my encounters at the Wall became too intense, as they often did, I crossed the Old City to my other favorite spectator perch, just outside the Damascus Gate. There, I watched an endless Arab procession: Bedouin women in embroidered dresses, balancing baskets of food on their heads; men nervously fingering worry beads or adjusting their *keffiyah* folds; young boys, careening on their two-wheeled carts through crowds of shoppers; schoolgirls, modestly wearing long pants beneath their striped smocks, chattering on their way home.

My meanderings through the Old City, through the vaulted Crusader alleys and past the bright rugs on outdoor display in the Muristan, always returned me to the Jewish Quarter. As if to calculate the worth of my day, I frequently bargained with Musa, an Arab construction worker, over the price of the ancient Roman and Jewish coins that his friends had pocketed from the excavations that morning. After protracted negotiations and the exchange of my dollars and his dinari, we finally reached our predictable equilibrium of two for a dollar.

Midway through the year, when Jerusalem had fully enveloped me in its history and mystery, I received the welcome news that I had been granted tenure at Wellesley. To my surprise (for the wait had been long), I was vaguely unsettled by the implications of this most privileged of life sentences. Was Wellesley College really where I wanted to be for thirty more years? By that time I would have taught the daughters of my current students. Could I abandon the narrow, winding alleys of Jerusalem, inexorably coaxing me back into the recesses of Jewish history?

Discussions with my Tel Aviv colleagues had already made me aware of my nagging uneasiness with American history. During our early weeks together, while I was an American novelty, they questioned me relentlessly about the latest obscure monograph, or the current research of the newest academic star. I did not yet appreciate their sense of academic isolation in Israel; I only knew that in the Jewish state, American history felt like an unwieldy encumbrance. I wanted the freedom to pursue other, suddenly more compelling, tasks of historical inquiry.

For Passover we were invited to the Seder of an elderly Dutch classicist from the Hebrew University. In his transplanted European home in Talbieh, the most refined of Jerusalem's neighborhoods, we joined his three sons and their families. I was far more intrigued by their intergenerational contrasts than by the Four Questions. The professor, a Holocaust survivor, was still thoroughly European in his starched white shirt and dark suit. He spoke gently through his bristly white beard. His Israeli-born sons, veterans of the wars of 1967 and 1973, were brashly assertive in their flashy sport shirts, unbuttoned to display hairy chests and gold medallions. Yet, loving respect flowed between father and sons, from the last generation of European Jews who, by some mysterious Jewish genetic alchemy, had created the first generation of Israeli sabras. I encountered endless variations on this theme. At a *moshav* near Beersheva, we were the guests of Hannah, who had flown to Israel from Yemen as a young girl on Operation Magic Carpet. In her finely embroidered Yemenite dress, she served us a traditional Sabbath meal. After several desserts, we were joined by her teenage daughter, who wore jeans and an Israeli peasant blouse. Dina already spoke some English; Hannah did not. Dina loved American music, and she could hardly contain her eagerness to jettison the Yemenite culture of her family.

Then there was Ruthie, the daughter of Kurdistani immigrants, who cleaned our apartment weekly. After diligently mopping our floors and beating our carpets, she went downtown to work as a legal secretary. She yearned to become a civil servant. She watched us—how we dressed, what we bought—with undisguised fascination. Finally, she invited us to visit her father, with whom she was locked in a fierce struggle over his refusal to permit her to serve in the army. He sat sunning himself in his undershirt, baggy trousers, and slippers, in the courtyard of the building in Talpiot where his seven children and assorted relatives lived. He gazed at us incomprehendingly, perhaps assuming that we were responsible for corrupting his daughter. I wanted to tell him that I had already seen her future, in the West, and that he had every reason to be alarmed.

A month before our departure, there was a sudden surge of Arab terrorism. In the Old City, Jews were stabbed and bombs exploded. A boatload of PLO terrorists landed on a Tel Aviv beach, murdering eight hostages in a seedy hotel. The United States launched a frenetic round of shuttle diplomacy, with Henry Kissinger applying relentless pressure on Israel to be less "intransigent." I felt secretly proud of Israeli determination not to yield to either Arab threats or American demands—and momentarily ashamed by the American flags that fluttered from Kissinger's motorcade as it raced past our apartment on its way to the Knesset.

But in the final frenzy of sorting and packing, I was too preoccupied to delve into such hopelessly tangled identity issues. My daughter Pammy and I, sharing the wish to leave something of ourselves behind, buried notes and trinkets in the nearby valley. On July 4, the last full day of our Jerusalem year, I relinquished my normal Friday morning walk through Zion Square for challah, the weekend newspaper, and flowers. Instead, I went to the Western Wall to say goodbye to Jerusalem. I exited from Jaffa Gate, an hour later, to the sound of screaming sirens. Ambulances, escorted by jeeps blanketed with soldiers, sped by. I hurried home to hear the news: a powerful bomb, concealed in a discarded refrigerator outside a hotel in Zion Square, had exploded. More than a dozen Jews had been killed; nearly a hundred were injured. But for the imminence of our departure, I might have been among them.

Not too many hours later, in Athens, I wandered forlornly in the cradle of Western civilization, wondering what it had to do with me. At the Israeli consulate, I asked a security guard for the most recent issue of the Jerusalem *Post*. Bemused, he telephoned inside; a moment later, I was handed a folded newspaper. It was a month old. Israel was behind me.

A new year at Wellesley always begins with a formal convocation. The faculty, robed in full academic regalia, is magisterial. Out of habit I participated, but the moment we entered the College chapel and filed beneath the stained glass windows to our pews, I realized that I had not only returned to the United States and to Wellesley, but to Christendom. Wellesley College had been founded a century earlier, "for the glory of God and the service of the Lord Jesus Christ." For years, every trustee and teacher was required to belong to an evangelical church. A donor, in her deed of gift for one of the first buildings, had expressed the wish that Wellesley students receive "a truly Christian education," the better to imitate "Him who 'came not to be ministered unto but to minister.' " Although more blatant forms of Christian triumphalism had receded from Wellesley life, these were not yet empty phrases. The admonition to minister, embossed as the College motto, was still a staple of ceremonial exhortations. As I gazed around the chapel, visions of St. Patrick's Cathedral and Oberlin Sundays filtered through the stained-glass saints.

A few weeks later, on Rosh ha-Shanah, I felt different tugs of discomfort. Teaching classes was inconceivable; but attending synagogue still was problematic. I compromised. With friends for support, I ventured to Memorial Church at Harvard, where Hillel held its High Holy day services. We arrived late, at the beginning of the majestic *Aleinu* prayer, just as the rabbi and *chazzan*, robed in long white *kittels*, prostrated themselves in a graphic reenactment of ancient Temple ritual. Despite my lingering aversion to religious rites, I was riveted.

Later in that academic year, Golda Meir came to Wellesley to receive an honorary degree. It was as curious an encounter as I could imagine. This unshakably stolid old woman, gruff and unpretentious ("the only man in my Cabinet," Ben-Gurion once said), was now surrounded by the prissy politeness of a Wellesley reception in her honor. I wondered whether even her secret meetings in Jordan with King Abdullah on the eve of Israeli independence had been as incongruous.

We chatted briefly about the respective pleasures of Jerusalem and Tel Aviv. When I asked her to inscribe her autobiography for my children she was momentarily puzzled by my daughter's name, for Pamela, in Hebrew, is a fruit. But it is, at least, easily spelled. Jeffrey's name was more difficult, for there is no soft "J" sound. She asked, brusquely, for his Hebrew name. "He has none," I replied with embarrassment, suggesting that she name him. She did: uncannily, she chose Yakov, my Hebrew name and my grandfather's.

The bicentennial of American independence that summer, a proud moment of national euphoria, was acutely uncomfortable for me. The celebration was lavishly orchestrated from Washington in an attempt to obliterate the stigma of Watergate and the disgrace of Richard Nixon's resignation. Vacationing on Martha's Vineyard, where everyone planned to gather at the Edgartown harbor for fireworks, I dug in my heels. We would go, instead, to the West Tisbury town hall to see the Beatles in "The Yellow Submarine." (To my astonishment, three other people made the same choice.) Afterward, I again declined the fireworks and returned, alone, to our house.

Flipping the radio dial, I was rewarded with a sudden news flash from Israel. Just a week earlier, Palestinian terrorists in Athens had hijacked an Air France plane en route from Tel Aviv to Paris, diverting it first to Libya and then to Uganda. There, a "selection," a process all too tragically familiar to Jews, had been made: most of the non-Israeli passengers were released, but eighty-three Israelis were detained as hostages. While the West wrung its hands helplessly, Israelis planned and executed a daring rescue at Entebbe, news of which had just then been broadcast. I could feel the exultation in Israel and in me. Finally, on July 4, 1976, there was something I could celebrate.

But that only made me wonder how the United States could sustain what Israel had nurtured. Hebrew school for my children, certainly, but they were nearly as unenthusiastic about it as I once had been. After a year in Israel they must have realized, as I did, how inadequate it was. Like most parents who sent children there, I knew all too little about what the teachers were trying to teach. How could I reinforce what I wanted my children to learn? I sensed the futility of the gesture.

We joined friends for Passover Seders, which invariably were excruciating. Usually, we submerged our Jewish selves to celebrate the liberation struggles of black Americans or Palestinians. The Seder always degenerated into a raucous dinner party. The *Haggadah* was a foreign text to all of us. None of us knew as much as the foolish son, how to ask even the most elementary questions.

My minimal gesture of observance, lighting Friday night candles, had already begun to isolate me within my own family. It symbolized the strains of a rapidly disintegrating marriage. The more estranged I felt, the more I craved a comforting Jewish enclosure, but the more avidly I embraced ritual, the further apart our family drifted. As the self-appointed custodian of rituals designed to bind Jewish families together, I felt ever more alone as I performed it.

Any Jewish observance puzzled my father. He had finally reconciled himself to my academic career, especially after a prominent *New York Times* review of one of my books prompted a flurry of newspaper profiles and television interviews. (He proudly accompanied me to one studio only to firmly admonish me, as I knew he would, not to say anything controversial.) But my nascent Judaism unsettled him. Both my parents had relinquished their Jewish family heritage—Orthodoxy on his side and Bund socialism on my mother's—and called it freedom. How could I challenge their trade-off?

Candle-lighting, at least, was a private act. But my beard was my public face. When, with renewed interest in our family history, I discovered the only surviving photograph of Jacob, my bushy-bearded, Orthodox patriarch from the old country, I understood my father's discomfort. Jewish was "foreign," yet there I was, his only son, undermining his effort to elude his European heritage. The more American camouflage I shed, the more incomprehending he was.

Along the way, I had begun to relinquish some vestigial American allegiances. For at least twenty years, my sole organizational affiliation had been with the American Civil Liberties Union. Its glorification of dissent provided legitimacy for my own disaffection from American political culture. I wrote a chapter for its history of First Amendment freedoms; and, in the '60s, I was among a tiny handful of university professors teaching courses on the history of civil liberties. I had proudly championed Roger Baldwin, the founding father of the ACLU, through a Brandeis commencement and, when he was past ninety, I took my children on a pilgrimage to his Chilmark summer home, where he regaled them with questions about Stuart Little.

In the spring of 1977, the American Nazi Party threatened to march in Skokie, Illinois, a Jewish community with a large concentration of Holocaust survivors. Suddenly, like many other American Jews, I confronted a conflict in my identity as a Jew and as a civil libertarian. Among most American Jews I knew, the identification of Judaism with liberalism had been a sacred tenet of our secular faith. I had taken pride in the identification of Jews with liberal causes, as though the Bill of Rights had been handed down at Sinai with the Ten Commandments. I probably believed that belonging to the ACLU made me a better Jew.

But as the American Nazis reawakened horrific memories in the Skokie survivors, I was torn between my commitment to freedom of speech and my commitment to Jews. The survivors knew better than anyone that Nazi ideas, words, and symbols had consequences that were infinitely more appalling and tragic than any limitation on the First Amendment. Who in their right mind, I wondered, would not have stifled freedom of speech in Germany to save six million Jews? If the liberal ideal of freedom of speech could not assure a society that was good for Jews, I wanted no part of it.

I was haunted by the observation of one Skokie survivor: "It's just like what happened in World War II right here in the United States. When [Jews] had to speak up, they were afraid to speak up." The only Jew who vigorously defended the survivors was a New York rabbi named Meir Kahane. But the Skokie Holocaust survivors, an atypical community of American Jews, fought back and kept the Nazis away—not because they were committed to liberalism but because they disregarded one of its fundamental tenets. Pained by the ACLU's insensitivity to the survivors, I was infuriated by the assignment of a Jewish lawyer to represent the Nazis. Along with 30,000 other members, I cancelled my membership.

Not long afterward, I made an uneasy commitment to accompany my son to Saturday morning services for an entire year, in anticipation of his forthcoming bar mitzvah. I knew that if Jeff and I did not do it together, it would not be done at all. But my own memories of bar mitzvah discomfort were still too acute for me to anticipate the experience with anything but tortured ambivalence. What little I may ever have known of the service had long since vanished; only fragments of *Ein Kelohanu* and *Adon Olam* remained, doubtless because they signalled the service's imminent end.

Our second service was more unsettling than the first, because the *gabbai* had spotted me as a familiar unfamiliar face. With his recognition, I knew that I would soon be summoned to recite the blessings for the reading of the Torah. I studied anxiously all the next week, until the Hebrew letters finally sorted themselves out from a chaotic blur into coherent words. As I had anticipated, I was called for an *aliya*. I felt Cantor Gorsky hovering nearby, but this time I did not stumble.

As my discomfort slowly ebbed, I found a soothing rhythm to our weekly ritual. The structure of the service, the protocols of observance, and occasional glimmers of insight into the Torah text that we read and discussed began to erode my resistance. Sharing the experience with Jeff even encouraged the fantasy that he might elude the unpleasant associations that had plagued me for thirty years. But I underestimated the impediments. He made it clear, as I once had, that a bar mitzvah was not an entry to Judaism but, for an indeterminate time, an exit from it.

To his surprise (and mine), my commitment actually deepened. During the summer, a small group of us—rarely many more than the required ten—kept the service going. I began to internalize the weekly rhythm; by mid-Friday, as though I was still keeping Jerusalem time, I felt my anticipation for *Shabbat* rising. When, one steamy Saturday morning, the tenth person never arrived, I was startled by my own disappointment.

My Jewish attachment had another source, more painful for me to acknowledge. With divorce impending, I searched for a buffer to the disintegration of my family. Jewish time and space offered a sanctuary of structure, ritual, and friendship. Its permanence, in contrast to the transience of my marriage, was reassuring. Connected to other Jews, I felt less alone.

That fall, for the first time, I experienced the entire season of High Holy Days, from Rosh ha-Shanah to Simchat Torah. As though to certify my commitment, I was recruited to help transport the Torah scrolls between Harvard buildings. A friend and I, each carrying a Torah wrapped in a *tallit*, walked through Harvard Yard at midday under the gaze of uncomprehending students. It was permissible to be a Jew at home; perhaps I might yet become a Jew on the street.

But before I could go forward I needed to go back, on a meandering historical journey into our family past. It was hardly coincidental that I began to reconstruct my family history the year that my father turned seventy-five, the year of my son's bar mitzvah, and the summer preceding my divorce. Suspended generationally between my father and my son, I was in transit from a vanished European past to an uncertain American future. My task, it seemed, was to rebuild Jewish connections that had atrophied from American exposure. As my own immediate family unraveled, I turned back toward the seamlessness of family history.

Family, by then, had come to mean my father's family. During my boyhood years, the very idea of family seemed alien. Later, during my prolonged struggle to elude my father's world of commerce and my mother's social strivings, I did what I could to escape. For years thereafter, my father and I circled warily around each other, in distant orbits. Quite inadvertently, my mother eased our reconciliation. As she tumbled into an abyss of debilitating mental illness, she united my father and me in shared anguish and mutual solace.

Now I wanted to give my father back his past—or, at least, a version of it that could satisfy my own yearning for family continuity. That meant a renewed search for Jacob, my missing grandfather. In any reconstruction of our family history, Jacob's departure from Romania marked the decisive transition. I knew the American story, but not its Eastern European antecedents. Those had been all but obliterated by the memory loss that children of immigrants inflicted upon themselves. I wanted to hear Jacob's voice once again.

Even as a historian, I was unprepared for the peculiar frustrations of my quest. My very first attempt to document Jacob's life became a paradigm for the elusiveness of everything that I wanted to know. I wrote to the Census Bureau for two schedules that would have included Jacob. To my surprise, given Jacob's disappearance from my own life, his name actually appeared on the 1910 and 1920 schedules. With his existence officially confirmed, I felt reassured. A seventy-year-old census had reconnected us.

Each schedule duly noted that Jacob and his parents were born in Romania (not exactly true); and that he could read and write "Jewish," which surely meant Yiddish. But there were evident discrepancies, even errors. In 1910, Jacob was listed as forty-five years old. Ten years later, he was only forty-eight. According to the 1910 census, he had immigrated in 1912; even if I corrected the obvious mistake to 1902, that was contradicted by the 1920 census, which reported his arrival a year earlier.

Once I took into account the uneasy encounter between an immigrant and a census-taker, the chronological imprecision was less troubling. Doubtless, language barriers, memory lapses, and transcription errors helped to explain the inconsistencies. Jacob was merely another body to be tallied, and his biographical details were relatively inconsequential.

The census records offered a skeletal outline that tended to confirm what I already knew about Jacob from my father. Jacob was an unskilled laborer. He first worked in a cigar factory and then as a railroad watchman. His family, always impoverished, frequently changed residences, usually because they were evicted for failure to pay the rent. The response to one question about naturalization did disturb me. In 1920, after nearly twenty years in the United States, Jacob Samuel Auerbach, Yankl Shlomo in "Jewish," still was classified as "alien."

The only other official document to confirm Jacob's life in the United States was his death certificate. It, too, mixed truth and conjecture. His parents, Mendel and Sarah of Romania, were correctly named. His most recent occupation, teamster, was accurate. But now, when it was too late to matter, he had been given still another birth year: 1872. Otherwise, it told only that on January 22, 1923, Jacob suffered a fatal "Fracture of skull due to being struck by automobile (Probably Accidental)." The proof of his death hurt me. It meant that my father had been right. Jacob never had come to visit me. I felt betrayed and sad.

One photograph of Jacob survived, my only direct glimpse of him. He is seated on a high-backed wooden chair in front of a brick and stone wall (the foundation of their house, my father recalled). Jacob is well dressed, for what obviously was the special occasion that prompted his only picture. His jacket is carefully buttoned; a black fedora rests on his knee. When I scrutinize the photo for clues about Jacob, I always find that he conceals more than he reveals. His left hand, for example, is hidden beneath his hat. The lower half of his face is shielded by a full, graying mustache and beard. The wrinkles that spread back from his eyes hint at a smile, but his eyes are too deeply recessed in shadow for me to be certain. He leans slightly to one side, almost informally. But he stares directly at the camera (or at his son, who photographed him). Strong and composed, he is my Old World patriarch. Now, as always, he remains a distant, silent presence.

As elusive as he is, our family history pivoted on his experience.

He was the last European, the first American. Joining the exodus of Eastern European Jews at the turn of this century, he abruptly redirected the pattern of centuries of Auerbach family life. With extraordinary courage (or desperation), he left everything behind for American promises. Until I could make sense of his life, I could hardly even frame, no less answer, the questions that puzzled me about my life as an American Jew.

Family names often provide important identity clues, so I began there. To my surprise, given the lack of distinction among my known ancestors, twenty Auerbachs were judged worthy of inclusion in the old *Jewish Encyclopedia*. Even though no evidence suggested that Jacob was descended from any of them, I was genuinely pleased to discover that the Auerbachs were identified as a family of scholars who traced their origins to Moses Auerbach, court Jew to the fifteenth-century bishop of Regensburg.

A branch of the Auerbach family—not ours as far as I could tell—settled in Vienna until 1670, when Rabbi Menachem Mendel, along with other Viennese Jews, was driven into exile. Resettled in Moravia (where my Jacob's father later lived), Rav Mendel became a prominent Talmudic authority. I felt a certain kinship with him, as I did with another feisty Auerbach, the Posen chief rabbi in the seventeenth century. His clashes with colleagues were said to demonstrate his "inflexible and fearless character." I also felt an author's empathy with Rabbi Samuel ben David Tebele Auerbach, a kabbalistic commentator who narrowly escaped pogroms in Lublin and Reiser only to have the *Encyclopedia* dismiss his tract, "Hesed Shemo El," as having "no value whatever."

By the eighteenth century, Auerbach rabbis were widely scattered in Russia, Poland, Austria, and Germany. One of them compiled an early Hebrew grammar; another wrote a history of Viennese Jewry. Rabbi Meir ben Isaac Auerbach, one of the last of the noteworthy family rabbis, became the chief rabbi of the Ashkenazi community in Jerusalem, where he died in 1878. Rabbi Aviezri Auerbach of Halberstadt joined the German *protestrabbiner* who condemned Zionism. The family ultimately produced its own historian, Siegfried, whose 1957 history was lugubriously weighted toward martyrology. He noted, with evident pride, that no male Auerbach had ever changed his name. (How, I wondered, could anyone prove that negative?) And, considering the endless family wanderings across Europe, he had every reason to conclude, with equivalent pride, that the real family home never was Germany, Austria, or Poland (or even Romania), but "Jewry and Judaism."

Jewish family names often had specific geographical, occupational, or even anatomical referents. Until the end of the eighteenth century, most European Jews used only their first name together with their father's. Beginning in Austria, and spreading rapidly through other emancipated communities, Jews were required to adopt permanent family names (the better to assure tax payments and military service). Last names were tangible symbols of their formal absorption into Christian society, their badge of identity in the modern nation state.

Some Jews retained their father's name (Mendelsohn); others were identified by their occupation (Goldschmidt), hair color (Schwartz), or even size (Gross). Many names (Danzig, Brody, Berlin) reflected places of origin. Auerbach was one of these. There are two towns named Auerbach in Germany: one at the edge of the Rhine Valley north of the old university town of Heidelberg; the other south of Leipzig, close to the border with the Czech and Slovak republics. It seems likely that some time during the half-century preceding Jacob's birth in the 1860s, his grandfather, or another relative living in or near one of the small German towns of Auerbach, adopted it as the family name.

For some of my ancestors, however, geography was too mundane a source of identity. A charming story, passed down through the generations, attributed the family name to a legend associated with the birth of Rashi, the great eleventh-century Talmudic scholar. While Rashi's mother was pregnant, she was walking through the narrow streets of her village. Suddenly, armed soldiers on horseback rounded a corner and galloped toward her. Twisting in a desperate effort to save her unborn child, she pressed herself against the wall of the nearest house. Its stones miraculously yielded to enclose and protect her. "Overboich" ("over the belly," in German) ultimately became Auerbach. According to legend, the indented wall, like the family name, still survives.

Rashi was an ideal ancestor, especially for rabbinical families with shaky credentials who wanted to climb the status ladder of piety and scholarship. He supposedly was descended from the grandson of Hillel the Great, the first-century Jerusalem sage who was a descendant of King David, from whose family the Messiah will some day come. It is a compelling legend of family origins, not because it is true but because it has endured. I learned of it from an Israeli cousin whose source was her two elderly aunts, Jacob's nieces. The old women intuitively realized that the legend preserved the family that recounted it. Its intergenerational retelling offers perpetual family rebirth in a cycle of love, faith, miracles, survival, and redemption. Proof of its historical accuracy is superfluous. It is a satisfying creation story.

Precisely when, or why, the family left Germany is unknown. Anti-Jewish riots in 1819, or again in the 1840s, may have impelled a flight to safety. Perhaps a private decision brought about by a marriage or a business failure accounted for the move. As far back as the collective family memory extends, the story begins with Shalom Yakov Auerbach, who married Anna and fathered twelve sons (appropriately, the number fathered by the biblical patriarch, Jacob). One of them, Mendel, born in the 1840s in Kishinev (Bessarabia), became Jacob's father. Nothing is known of Shalom Yakov and little of his family. His sons scattered, early and widely, probably to avoid a lifetime of military service in the czar's army. Anna, late in her life, apparently made a gallant effort to locate them. Her search ended, with unknown results, in the Land of Israel, where she died and was buried in Safed.

Mendel evidently returned home to Kishinev, the thriving industrial and commercial center of Bessarabia. There, just inside the southeastern edge of the Pale of Jewish settlement, he worked as the representative of a German coffee company. From his business contacts, Mendel may have developed an astute sense of the precariousness of Bessarabian Jewry. Even before the assassination of Czar Alexander in 1881 unleashed a wave of devastating pogroms, government decrees had narrowly restricted the areas of Jewish settlement and imposed heavy fines on Jews who resisted military service. Mendel and his wife Feige left Kishinev, moving one hundred miles west, across the Prut River to the Moldavian city of Botosoni. There they raised their family: a son (Jacob) and four daughters (Shifra, Pauline, Yetty, and Oltilia). Mendel, according to one of his granddaughters, was greatly admired in the community. When he died, while still in his early forties, "everybody from his street closed the business to give him respect."

The city of Botosoni, where Jacob and his sisters grew up, was the second largest in Moldavia, with important trade connections to Brody and Leipzig. Most of its merchants and artisans and half its population of 33,000 were Jews. The Jewish community, dating from the early sixteenth century, had experienced the normal range of anti-Semitic hostility. For a time, Moldavian Jews had been treated as lepers; Christians could not touch what they touched or eat what they ate. Restricted to certain neighborhoods, Jews were required to wear black clothing and pay exorbitant taxes. Accusations of ritual murder triggered periodic violence. At the Congress of Berlin (1878) where Romania received independence, Jews were promised full civil rights. Despite these assurances, they still were denied the privileges of citizenship and treated as inferior aliens.

Toward the end of the century, conditions rapidly deteriorated. Poor harvests depressed the economy, restrictive occupational laws were enacted, Jewish students were expelled from public schools, synagogues were desecrated, and riots erupted in Botosoni and nearby shtetls. At the end of May, 1899, a pogrom swept through Jassy, the largest Jewish community in Moldavia, just sixty-five miles from Botosoni. It prompted an unparalleled wave of migration known as the "Romanian exodus." Within little more than a decade, one-third of Romanian Jewry emigrated to the United States. They were led by the *fusgeyer* ("foot-walkers"), groups of desperate, hopeful young men and women who pooled their meager resources and set out for the port of Hamburg, one thousand miles away. For safety and sustenance they traveled in groups of one hundred or more, buoyed by the food and prayers they received from Jewish communities along their route.

Their courage doubtlessly emboldened many who were not so young or romantic. From Bucharest, Jassy, Galatz, and Braila by foot, train, and Danube steamer, tens of thousands of Romanian Jews followed in their wake. Rapidly, according to one historical narrative, "the fever of emigration transformed itself into a delirium. All the Jews wanted to leave . . . the hellish country in which life had become intolerable." Jacob Auerbach was among them. By then he was married to Minnie Bergman, a young woman just past twenty from the nearby village of Piatra Neamt. Her parents, Calman and Mischka, owned a family business that had fallen on hard times. Minnie already had a son (perhaps from a brief previous marriage); her first child with Jacob, a daughter, was born around the turn of the century.

Jacob's decision to emigrate alone could not have been easy. But times were desperate. And a family member, Israel Cohen, brother-in-law of Jacob's sister Yetty, lived in Pittsburgh. He probably encouraged Jacob to leave Romania. Perhaps he also sent thirty-four dollars, the cost of ship passage. Some time in 1901, the second year of the Romanian exodus (a five-year period when 6,000 Jews emigrated annually), Jacob left Botosoni. Perhaps Minnie, in her sorrow, sang this popular lullaby to their baby daughter:

> *Where did father go, mother dear?*
> *He went to find bread, to earn money,*
> . . . .
> *He went to America. . . .*
> *Why so far away?*
> *Here, mother, in this place*
> *Is there no bread for us?*

Jacob's journey from Botosoni was hazardous. Immigrants deemed "unsuitable" by a border or health official could be turned back. Hundreds of homeless Jews without money to continue their travels set up camp in an old cemetery in Galatz. If an immigrant did not already possess ship passage, it could take months of work to pay for the trip. (One Romanian Jew in Pittsburgh recalled crossing the border into Austria, working for two weeks, then traveling to Bremerhaven, where it took him three months of manual labor to purchase his fare.) The men traveled lightly; their personal possessions might only include their *siddur*, *tallit*, and *t'fillin*. They relied upon Jews in Bukovina and Transylvania to provide food and shelter along the way.

From Vienna, Romanian Jews usually continued to Rotterdam, perhaps to Hamburg or Bremen. If they were fortunate, they might receive assistance from the *Alliance Israelite Universelle* or the Jewish

Colonization Association. But these philanthropic agencies, while sympathetic to the plight of the immigrants, were apprehensive about the mass influx of Jews to the United States. In 1900, Jacob Schiff, the prominent American banker and philanthropist, suggested that Romanian Jews consider other destinations; and the New York Romanian Committee, complaining about the arrival of so many "beggars," urged a monthly quota of only two hundred newcomers.

In 1901, the year of Jacob's departure, the philanthropic agencies became more selective. The *Alliance*, for example, instructed its representatives to choose only young, healthy, and skilled Jews for emigration. The newly appointed agent of the Jewish Colonization Association for Romania, a German Jew named Wolfgang Auerbach, was advised to approve only unmarried males or husbands who would agree to leave their families behind. Between May and September he sent thirty-two groups (738 immigrants) to the United States.

Perhaps Wolfgang Auerbach helped Jacob to leave for America. Jacob certainly qualified: he was still a relatively young man, he had left his wife and child behind, he had an American relative to help him, and he was healthy and eager to work. If his fare was already paid by Israel Cohen, that made it easier for him. But the selection process could be random; perhaps the coincidence of a common family name eased Jacob's departure.

When Jacob left Europe, the ocean crossing no longer was as perilous as it once had been. The voyage took days, not weeks or months. Shipboard conditions varied, according to another Romanian Jew bound for Pittsburgh, from "awful to bearable." Steerage was crowded, and passengers were forced to endure a babel of languages and the rancid smells of food and waste. The more fortunate travelers ate herring and potatoes, nibbled hard cheese, and drank bean soup and coffee. If Jacob had traveled with Romanian *landsmen*, he could have joined them in song and card-playing, sharing reminiscences and yearnings to allay their trepidation.

Jacob probably arrived at Ellis Island, which became the major immigrant processing center after 1892. All newcomers, arranged by nationality, were questioned by multilingual inspectors about their mental competence, political beliefs, work prospects, and family contacts. They underwent dreaded medical examinations for contagious and "loathsome" diseases. If Jacob was fortunate, he was met by an agent of the Hebrew Immigrant Aid Society or the Romanian Hebrew Aid Society, who directed him to the Manhattan ferry, found a place for him to spend the night, and guided him to the railroad station for his overnight trip to Pittsburgh.

First encounters with Pittsburgh invariably were disappointing. Its sprawling iron and steel factories spewed smoke and soot across the city. (I remembered that from childhood visits to my grandmother.) Immigrants described the city as "dark, dismal and dirty"; "so dark"; "dirty, unattractive, smoky"; "smoky and dirty." But the mill jobs in Pittsburgh were a magnet for unskilled laborers from Southern and Eastern Europe. Some 14,000 Jews already lived there (the number tripled within a decade of Jacob's arrival), crowded into a downtown neighborhood known as the Hill district. Jews were interspersed among Poles, Russians, Lithuanians, Hungarians, Italians, and Ukrainians in a pulsating, expanding immigrant ghetto. Romanian Jews, the most recent arrivals, were the most impoverished.

Jacob's train from New York arrived at the B&O station, where Israel Cohen would have greeted him. It was not a long walk to his new American home, a neighborhood of crowded row houses, which "seemed to sweat humanity at every window and door." Its main streets were jammed with horse-drawn wagons and lined with kosher butchers and bakeries, fish stores displaying their stock of herring and carp in sidewalk barrels, second-hand clothing stores, pawnshops and nickelodeons. There were pushcart peddlers everywhere, shouting for (and at) customers, exhorting them to buy used clothing, mismatched shoes, and discarded pots and pans. Perhaps Israel took Jacob to an ice-cream parlor on Liberty Avenue to discuss family news, living arrangements, and work prospects. In those hectic first days, Jacob, like other newcomers to the city, probably visited Kalson's bath house before settling into his new quarters, usually a room shared with other boarders. Soon he began to work in Israel Cohen's stogy factory.

"What could I do in Pittsburgh?," an immigrant asked. "Make stogies. So I learned the stogy trade." The Pittsburgh tobacco industry—meaning the manufacture of cheap cigars from tobacco leaves stuffed with filler—was the largest single source of employment for Jewish immigrants. In the Hill district alone, nearly one hundred and fifty shops provided temporary employment for thousands of newcomers who were desperate for work and willing to endure daily misery to earn a weekly pittance.

Many of the shops were located in basements, attics, or spare rooms. From 7 A.M. until 6 P.M. (except on the Sabbath), workers cut the leaves and rolled the stogies, inhaling tobacco dust in unventilated rooms. Even on the hottest days, all the windows were closed to prevent the leaves from blowing away. There was an acrid stench from tobacco and sweat. The wages (twenty-five to thirty dollars a month for adult men; ten dollars for women and boys) barely covered the cost of room and board. But the work, requiring no skill, was quickly learned. And, as bad as the stogy sweatshops were, at least they were closed on Jewish holy days. Children as young as nine, whose earnings were desperately needed by their families, could work there to supplement the family's income. Yet, one Jew wondered, "So what is the use of coming to America, to Pittsburgh, to be a stogy roller who worked like a slave?"

Jacob, too, must have worked long hours, for within a year he was able to bring Minnie and their daughter Leona from Romania. Their first American child, Mendel, died soon after birth, but in August, 1903, Minnie gave birth to another son. He was named Menachem Moshe, in memory of his paternal grandfather and to commemorate Shabbat Nachumu, the first Sabbath of consolation after Tisha b'Av, the week before his birth. Menachem Moshe was Americanized to M. Maurice and then abbreviated to Morry, the name by which everyone knew my father. The family, enlarged by another son and a daughter, lived in a frame house on Rowley Street. Boarders occupied the second floor and Jacob's stogy factory was in the attic. After some years of struggle, they escaped to the grass and trees of Devilliers Street, a Hill neighborhood preferred by the more settled immigrants.

By then, the Hill had a range of Jewish communal institutions. Weinstein's kosher restaurant was open around the clock; Hirsch's bookstore sold Yiddish books and newspapers; there was a Yiddish theatre, the Irene Kaufman settlement house, and two Romanian shuls: Or Chodesh and Ohel Jacob. After the Russians and Lithuanians, the Romanian community was the largest. But its economic base remained precarious. The stogy industry was wracked by incessant labor conflict over its abysmal wage scale. In 1913, more than a thousand Jewish stogy workers went out on strike. Employers held firm and, after a four-month strike, the industry was badly crippled. Many shops closed; those that survived hired young Polish and black women to assure a more compliant work force. Jacob's stogy factory was probably a casualty of the strike.

Jacob then found work as a railroad watchman. His oldest son, barely ten, sold newspapers and shined shoes. It must have been a difficult time. Morry never lost the memory of his father packing a kosher meal to take to the train yards for his frequent Sabbath absences from home. And, after seventy-five years, his sister Anne still recalled their mother lighting the Sabbath candles, always a prelude to her sorrowful weeping at the weekly reminder of her parents in Europe whom she would never see again.

There were, to be sure, happy family memories, among them Jacob's passion for Romanian music and his melodious voice. ("A *chazzan's* voice," Anne remembered.) His stern attendance requirements at *shul* were less welcome but dutifully obeyed, especially on the High Holy Days. Perhaps there was even some comfort in measuring American possibilities against Romanian realities. In 1907, a Jewish immigrant in Pittsburgh recalled, there was a pogrom in Botosani. "Jews were robbed and murdered."

In Pittsburgh, Jews were safe from pogroms, but not immune to random tragedy. Early in the evening of January 22, 1923, Jacob, by then employed as a teamster, was driving a horse-drawn bakery wagon on his delivery rounds. Struck broadside by an automobile, he was flung to the street and suffered a fractured skull. Without regaining consciousness, he died that night at Mercy Hospital and was buried the next day in the Kasa Torah cemetery.

That was all I could learn about Jacob's life. I scrutinized the few artifacts that my father passed along to me, as though they would reveal what else I might want to know. I have Jacob's gold-plated, pocket-watch chain. I wish that it was visible in my photograph of Jacob, but it is not. I also have two pairs of silver serving forks and spoons, engraved with Jacob's initials. I feel bonded to him by our identical "JSA." There is his *t'fillin* bag, a parting gift from his father-in-law, whose initial is enclosed in a wreath of embroidered flowers. Finally, there is a silver spice-box, delicately filigreed and crowned with a flag. I can easily imagine Jacob, during the *havdalah* ceremony that marks the end of the Sabbath, holding it to bless the spices inside, a fragrant reminder of the departing day of rest. Even now, as my young daughters eagerly sniff its aroma, I feel our family circle widen across the generations to include my missing grandfather.

As attached as I am to these few family possessions, they cannot begin to answer questions that I wish I could have asked Jacob: What did your father, Mendel, tell you about his father and grandfather? How could you leave everyone—wife, child, four sisters—behind? Did you ever consider following your grandmother Anna to the Land of Israel? Did America fulfill any of its promises, or did twenty years of menial work and poverty, and Minnie's unassuaged yearning for those she left behind (including the son who did not rejoin her for ten years), make you regret your decision to emigrate? Did those Romanian folk songs that you sang, with such bittersweet fervor that your children still remembered the beauty of your voice after seventy-five years, express some ineradicable nostalgia? Why Romanian, and not Yiddish, songs?

Without answers to these questions, there is the temptation to create Jacob in the likeness of my fantasies. I am free to see in Jacob what I want to believe about him, not who he was. But I feel bound by the silence of his life to respect his anonymity. I try to draw meaning from that. He left Romania. He came to the United States. He fathered our American family. If that was all, that was something. I cannot get closer to him than that. Nor, however, can I elude him.

Minnie, like Jacob, remained a stranger in a strange land. She never learned to speak English; she lost a child within a year of her arrival; after Jacob's death, she was reduced to complete dependence upon her sons. As far as I know, she never ventured outside Pittsburgh. I have no indication that her life in the United States ever provided more than a rare moment of solace, at most, to compensate for all her suffering. My older cousins, with whom she lived when they were young girls, have told me that she was always remote, even cold. Even as we light the candles in Minnie's brass candlesticks, I am reminded of the pain inflicted upon her by her life in the United States.

Jacob and Minnie, the immigrants, endured lives of privation. Still relatively young when they arrived, they never eked out more than a bare subsistence. As caring as their children were, they had their own lives to live as Americans. The shtetl culture of their parents was an unwelcome intrusion that the children rejected as quickly as possible. I still wonder whether Pittsburgh, for my grandparents, was any improvement over Botosoni.

Jacob's sisters remained behind in Romania. They married; three bore children. They managed, somehow, to survive the Holocaust that destroyed half of Romanian Jewry. After the war, Yette— like Jacob half a century earlier—joined another Romanian exodus, this time to Israel. What if Jacob, too, had stayed behind? Perhaps, if he had, I might not be here to ask the question. Or I might have grown up like my cousin Zippi, Pauline's granddaughter, who emigrated from Italy to Israel with her mother after the war. Now her family, daughters and grandchildren alike, are Israelis. In Israel, Auerbach family roots are deeply entwined with the future of the Jewish state.

Jacob remains my only link, fragile as it is, to the lost world of Eastern European Jewry. Long before shtetl culture was demolished by modernity or annihilated by the Nazis, Jacob abandoned it. He made the fateful decision that still controls our family destiny. Because he chose the United States, our family history stops, and starts, with him. Before Jacob, I cannot know anything with certainty, for immigration meant obliteration. There is only Irving Howe's bittersweet epitaph for the world of our fathers: "Let us now praise obscure men." If they did nothing else, they endured. And they continue to haunt our memories.

Jacob's legacy, filtered through my father, remains elusive. Whatever accompanied Jacob from Romania vanished without a trace, with only the vigor of my father's denial to suggest what might once have been. Not Jacob's Orthodoxy, nor even any vestiges of *yiddishkeit* (beyond a superstitious phrase or two), survived the chill of assimilation that settled across the second generation. If Jacob was the prototypical Jewish immigrant, my father personified the ambivalence of second-generation American Jews. Too rooted in Judaism to deny it, he was too uneasy to assert it.

Some of this is evident from the photographs of his early years. The smallest boy in his grammar school graduation class, he was in transition to American respectability. His double-breasted jacket was buttoned; his knickers were trim; only his open shirt collar, flopping conspicuously over his jacket lapels (the other boys wore ties), indicated that he was not quite there yet. But by his mid-teens, just after World War I, the boyhood scruffiness was gone. A member of the "Minyun Klub of Pittsburgh"—the name itself a revealing Americanization of the congregation required for Jewish prayer—he was strikingly handsome with dark wavy hair, a starched collar, and a tie.

Within another year, he was a dashing blade. Photographs from the 1920s display his attentiveness to sartorial fashion. In one picture he wears a striped shirt with a floppy bow-tie; in another, seated on the hood of a Model T, he is dressed in knickers and gaudy knee socks; among a group of male friends he wears a polo coat and fedora that match theirs; with a girl friend he is dapper in a suit and vest; and at a friend's wedding he seems comfortable in a top hat and white gloves.

Even these photos, taken long before I was born, offer some familiar glimpses of my father: his stylishness (I was always amazed by the sheer quantity of suits, shirts, ties and shoes that he owned), and his evident warmth. A social person, he enjoyed good times with many friends. Indeed, he seems far happier in these earlier pictures than I remember him. He looks self-assured, with traces of exuberance that were long gone by the time he became a parent and the Great Depression became a metaphor for the mood that hovered over our family. By early adulthood, he had transformed himself from a street urchin, hustling to sell newspapers and shine shoes on Pittsburgh street corners, into a stylish Jazz Age bachelor.

In the process, of course, he was becoming an American. Just as there was little to distinguish Jacob from millions of other Eastern European Jews (he emigrated, he struggled, he died), so my father, like countless other American-born children of immigrant parents, dedicated his life to eradicating every remnant of Old

World culture. He became that distinctive hybrid, a second-generation American Jew, precariously in transition from the stifling Orthodoxy of his parents to American respectability.

What my father learned, and practiced with true artistry, was how to remain enclosed within exclusively Jewish surroundings without ever identifying with anything Jewish. Wherever he lived, worked, or vacationed, the story repeated itself. He carefully located himself between Jewish identification and American assimilation.

It still amazes me how adeptly my father navigated these menacing shoals of Jewish identity and how, with unerring accuracy, he always managed to find other Jews who were exactly like him. Perhaps he convinced himself—certainly he could not have persuaded any Gentile—that he had erased whatever distinguished him from "genuine" Americans. It was, of course, precisely his finely calibrated internal balance of accommodation that marked him, quite conspicuously, as a second-generation American Jew. He was obliged to repudiate his father's legacy to protect his son's future.

That must be why everyone I knew, from kindergarten through high school, had parents just like mine. None of us could elude the second-generation constraints that our parents imposed upon us. Their assimilationist straitjacket fit as comfortably as our baseball gloves and baggy sweatshirts. We were never more certain of our freedom than when, as the good Jewish boys we were, we internalized parental acculturation priorities.

Wellesley College finally undermined my commitment to these terms of American Jewish accommodation. After a decade, I thought I had more or less made my peace with the anomalies of my presence in a women's college. I knew that I could never identify with the institution with the fervor displayed by my female colleagues, especially those—and there were many—whose loyalties extended back to their own undergraduate infatuation with its gothic towers and manicured lawns. The college was their community, indeed their life.

But it was only my workplace. There, I had learned that an ostensible commitment to "feminism," in translation, meant little more than preparing young women for the same high-paying jobs, in banks and law firms, that privileged men had traditionally monopolized. I found cloying the entrenched institutional fondness for genteel manners at the expense of intellectual daring, for therapeutic nurturing rather than critical thinking. I knew that I was doubly incongruous: a Jewish male intruding upon Christian female space.

For a time, I had shrugged aside occasional infelicities of expression that I might have taken more seriously. One day, while lunching with a colleague whose name (Cohen) left no doubt that he was Jewish, we were joined by the college president. Our superficial similarities—we were both Jews, in our forties, with beards—must have momentarily disoriented her, for she blithely inquired whether we were cousins.

Similar malapropisms punctuated faculty meetings. The president so routinely called me "Pinsky" and my colleague Pinsky "Auerbach" that he and I jocularly began to address each other by her inversions. Then there was the time, after I announced my intention to teach a seminar on American Jewish history, when a colleague nagged me to "broaden" it into a course on immigration, as though the natural destiny of Jews was to become indistinguishable from everyone else.

But my tolerance had its limits, and the inauguration of President Nan Keohane finally exceeded them. The normal somnolence of academic pomp was rudely interrupted, for me, when everyone joined in singing a hymn that could only have come from a Protestant psalter. (Instantly I recalled Oberlin's "Father, Son and Holy Ghost.") Then, as the new president received the symbolic keys to her position, I realized for the first time that the spiritual life of Wellesley College was symbolized by the Christian cross. So parochial a symbol, framing an inaugural lecture devoted to Wellesley's ostensible commitment to pluralism and diversity, began to rouse me from silent acquiescence.

A colleague had recently alerted me to admissions data and presidential correspondence in the college archives that demonstrated Wellesley's historical fondness for Jewish quotas. The Admissions Office had once made "a conscious effort," in its own words, to limit the number of Jewish students—for their own good, it claimed. Jews had been classified among those groups "characterized by identifiable physical features," although which parts of their anatomy were especially revealing was discreetly left unsaid. The director of admissions, who had been at Wellesley long enough to have inherited and endorsed the pattern of Jewish restriction, was not pleased when I cited the quota statistics at a faculty meeting. Nor did she seem to appreciate my suggestion, at a private meeting in her office, that an effort could be made to enlist the support of Jewish students in recruiting qualified Jewish newcomers. Any such "change in policy," she responded testily, must come from higher college sources. Until then, Wellesley would remain committed to its policy of geographical distribution, which benignly assured the continued underrepresentation of Jewish students (whose families were not inclined to cluster in Utah, New Mexico, Idaho, Montana, or the Dakotas). I could hardly have received more reliable evidence, from a more informed source, that Wellesley still had a Jewish problem.

My emerging reputation as Wellesley's "Jew" made me the repository for a spate of additional documentation. Jewish students reported anti-Semitic slurs whenever Israel did something unpopular, which was often. They told me how the admissions office steered its recruiters away from predominantly Jewish high schools. I learned about instructors who were insensitive to the religious observance of their Jewish students, even on Yom Kippur. And I heard from a colleague, visiting an introductory history class during a discussion of seventeenth-century anti-Semitism, who was startled to hear students affirm precisely the venerable anti-Semitic canards that they were studying.

President Keohane, under duress, finally circulated a memo to the faculty linking Yom Kippur to Good Friday as a "High Holy Day," when work was forbidden to the religiously observant. (If there ever had been a complaint about faculty insensitivity on Good Friday, no one knew about it.) Even after the local Anti-Defamation League office expressed its concern to the college, she could only bring herself to acknowledge a problem about "perceptions" of Wellesley, as though there was nothing in reality to substantiate them.

Wellesley being Wellesley, even its anti-Semitism was genteel.

But there remained one pocket of festering anti-Semitic prejudice, which had been all but institutionalized within the Department of Religion. The department still was an unofficial, but vigilant, guardian of the Christian exclusiveness of the founders' vision of Wellesley. In the entire history of the college, it had never granted tenure to a Jew. Only Christians, presumably, could teach the Bible without religious faith subverting their scholarly objectivity. Jewish scholars might, occasionally, be hired temporarily to teach the "Old Testament," as the Hebrew Bible was smugly labeled, but never the New.

As untenable as such prejudices had become in polite society, they still endured at Wellesley into the 1980s. Then an exceedingly talented young Bible scholar (and an Orthodox Jew) came up for tenure. The department prepared a paper trail of smarmy allegations about his lack of sociability (which often meant no more than his unwillingness to violate Jewish holy days to attend departmental functions). His splendid scholarship was more difficult to impeach, but the department tried. The candidate, in a gesture of scholarly ecumenicism, had submitted the names of three potential evaluators: a Protestant, a Catholic, and a Jew. His tenured colleagues instructed him to replace at least two with others drawn from their own list of six (compiled, they claimed, to assure diversity)—all of whom were Protestants teaching in theology seminaries. When he balked at their proposal, they branded him an "unusually difficult colleague" and denied him tenure.

Declining to play with their stacked deck, he retained legal counsel. With enough damning documentation of departmental anti-Semitism to assure judicial scrutiny, and no end of unfavorable publicity along the way, President Keohane intervened to encourage reconsideration. While all this festered, in 1983, I happened to read an essay in *Commentary* about the secret anti-Semitic life of Sarah Lawrence College. It recounted episodes that so precisely replicated the Wellesley pattern as to nearly convince me that there was a case of mistaken institutional identity. In a letter to the editor, I submitted my own postscript drawn from Wellesley data. Published several months later, it touched a raw nerve among Wellesley colleagues, alums and trustees, who rushed into print to exonerate the college.

I was fascinated, in a gloomy sort of way, by the evasive ingenuity of their responses. Some, believing that progress is inevitable, insisted that Wellesley must be more tolerant than it once had been. Others conceded the presence of prejudiced individuals at the college, but carefully differentiated their behavior from institutional anti-Semitism (even when some of the most prejudiced individuals just happened to have been presidents, admissions officers, and department chairmen).

Then there were those who insisted that Wellesley was no worse than other elite schools, which certainly was as true as the fact that it was no better (and much less willing than Yale or Princeton to make amends). Others parroted Wellesley's commitment to tolerant diversity, as though anti-Semitic quotas did not in any way contradict their claim. One Jewish trustee even inquired, discreetly, what I might regard as the "appropriate" percentage of Jewish students at Wellesley, if twelve percent was too low. She seemed genuinely surprised when I proposed only a meritocratic admissions process.

President Keohane blithely insisted that her predecessors had acted in "everyone's" best interest. But she declined to indicate how restrictive quotas might have served the best interest of Jews. She conceded, however, that prior rationalizations might now "seem" unacceptable—appearances, at Wellesley, often providing the only reality. Furthermore, such unpleasant "insensitivities," as she delicately labeled them, belonged to ancient history—as remote, in some instances, as the preceding academic year.

I was, if anything, more enraged by the polite evasions and denials than by the episodes themselves. My Jewish colleagues, predictably, were annoyed with me for my public criticism. When I told them of my intention to provoke a full discussion of Wellesley anti-Semitism at a faculty meeting, they were furious. Any discussion of anti-Semitism, they surely realized, would necessarily implicate them. After so many years in hiding, they would finally be exposed as Jews.

Faculty meetings at Wellesley are preceded by an elaborate ritual of decorum, designed to emphasize the priority of good manners over substantive issues. Tea is poured from elegant silver pitchers into sparkling china cups. Platters of cookies, adequate but never ample, are circulated. Teacups, cookies, and conversations are decorously balanced. After twenty minutes, faculty members proceed to a cavernous wood-paneled room divided down the middle like the House of Lords. There, I shattered the polite silence to insist that Wellesley anti-Semitism be confronted and condemned. When I went public, I became an unwitting participant in a larger Jewish drama. In their two-century-long struggle for civic equality, Jews had often displaced their discomfort in a hostile Gentile world upon each other. Endemic to modern Jewish history was the conflict between assimilated Western Jews, eager for Christian approval, and unenlightened Eastern Europeans, still clinging tenaciously to their shtetl ways. So it still was at Wellesley. Our debate, predictably, was between Jews. For weeks, my colleagues agonized whether or not to acknowledge, and then actually condemn, anti-Semitism. Would we recognize it as an institutional, nor merely an individual, problem? Would the continuity between past and present anti-Semitism at Wellesley be recognized?

My archetypical opponents in this debate—the Moral Jew, the Silent Jew, and the Court Jew—responded with resounding negatives to each question. The Moral Jew sincerely regretted past infelicities at the college. But the problems of Jews were minor compared to what other suffering minorities, from Afganistan to Zaire, still endured. To focus exclusively on anti-Semitism, now that Jews were so privileged, was an unseemly distraction. Not anti-Semitism alone, but every known form of discrimination—or none—must be condemned.

Then there was the Silent Jew, who sat wordlessly through our interminable discussions. In a post-Holocaust world, I wondered, how could Jews remain mute about anti-Semitism in their own workplace? I knew the fear of retribution at tenure time inhibited junior colleagues. Tenured colleagues, however, were not at risk. Perhaps they were as remote from Judaism as I once had been, or were determined to be Jews only in the privacy of their homes and synagogues. The silence of so many saddened me.

As an erstwhile Silent Jew and Moral Jew, I could recognize my earlier self in colleagues of those persuasions. But the Court Jew, so desperately eager to be aligned with College authorities, aroused my deepest contempt. I listened to the resident rabbi bless the president and the admissions office for their repentance and urge our forgiveness—weeks before the issue even was debated. A senior colleague, normally too devoted to his research center even to attend meetings, roused himself long enough to invest the president and trustees with the wisdom and courage seldom attributed to divine-right monarchs. Even by prevailing standards of academic subservience and capitulation, it was disgusting.

After prolonged equivocation, the faculty finally decided to condemn anti-Semitism and all other forms of racial and religious prejudice. Wearily, we invited the president and trustees to affirm these bland universalist principles, wrung from endless hours of acrimonious debate. But the trustees, led all too predictably by their handful of Jewish members, declined. Instead, they deleted all references to Jews and anti-Semitism, affirmed Wellesley's mythical "history of dedication to diversity," and pledged their allegiance to the "the moral imperative of the Founders." That imperative, of course, was precisely the source of the Christian exclusivity that accounted for Wellesley's continuing Jewish problem.

As the furor over anti-Semitism finally subsided, the college felt increasingly like a foreign country. Unlike Groucho Marx, I had no desire to belong to a club that did not want me as a member. Wellesley had become the repository for all my uncomfortable feelings as a Jew in the United States.

IT WAS A ZIONIST CATASTROPHE, MANY AMERICAN JEWS believed, when Menachem Begin was elected Prime Minister of Israel in 1977. Begin challenged the axiom of modern Jewish politics, the identification of Judaism with liberalism. An Eastern European shtetl Jew, he reminded westernized Jews (all too uncomfortably) of their Old World antecedents. With a didactic tendency to recite Holocaust lessons endlessly and occasionally inappropriately, Begin nonetheless knew how to frame Zionist issues within the larger sweep of Jewish history. I found it refreshing that Israel finally had a prime minister who was sufficiently comfortable as a Jew to wear a *kipa* and pray at the Western Wall.

Amid the rising discomfort of American Jews with the Jewish state, Israel pulled at me relentlessly. The frequency of my visits increased, as I replenished my Jewish resources for another year of spiritual exile. I found myself tracking the footsteps of the ancient Israelites, whose wilderness wanderings, from Ur and then from Egypt, brought Abraham to Hebron and King David from there, finally, to Jerusalem.

My own pilgrimage began in the silent spaciousness of Sinai, where the Israelites had been forged into a nation bound by law and tempered by adversity for their entry into the promised land. In the prophecy of Hosea, I read: "I will allure [Israel], and bring her into the wilderness, and speak tenderly to her . . . as in the day when she came up out of the land of Egypt." There, where Jewish history began, I might locate my own place within it.

The modern journey to Sinai passes through Eilat, the nearest Israeli equivalent, I imagined, to the biblical Sodom. But desert rhythms are soothing and, with almost frightening suddenness, completely enclosing. In Sinai, space was everywhere, but familiar boundaries of time collapsed. Each day became many days: the early morning chill in the shadowy canyons of the jagged red mountains before sunrise; the swelling, unremitting heat of the parched, bleak desert in midday; the palpable rejuvenation, as the heat subsided in the lengthening late afternoon shadows; the blackness of night, when a sliver of moonlight fully illuminated the craggy landscape.

Sinai relentlessly demands conformity to its own unalterable rhythms. Resistance is futile; energy, like water, must be conserved. My companion guides, the Bedouin, intuitively understood this. Compared to the ancient Israelites, who murmured their incessant grievances once they exchanged slavery for freedom, the Bedouin have adapted to survive. Their effortless efficiency transforms the most mundane activity—packing camels or baking *labneh*, rinsing coffee cups or cutting toothpicks—into a series of swift, spare, silent gestures.

The wilderness imposes its own nuances of status, subtleties of communication, and obligations of reciprocity. One evening, in the gathering darkness, I witnessed a ritualized exchange of visits among Bedouin from different tribes. Each came, in turn, to the camp of the other, gathering by the fire to share food, drink, cigarettes and conversation. Reclining on one elbow or squatting with their weight forward, white *keffiyahs* and leggings accenting their dark skin, they were relaxed yet alert. They could uncoil instantly to chase a straying camel, anticipating its every move until their gracefully choreographed collaboration finally cornered it. I listened to the Bedouin chant their wailing songs, piercing the desert stillness with their ancient memories and longings.

The night before I climbed Mt. Sinai, beneath the "star-seeded" desert sky that Thomas Mann described so evocatively, I felt the force of the wilderness in the rushing howl of the wind sweeping through the dry *wadi*. The desert was abrasive, yet cleansing; it could destroy mercilessly, yet it shaped a resilient people. The children of Israel had to submit to its majestic power to learn what was demanded of them for life in their promised land. At the summit of the mountain, as the sun's first rays spread rosy light across the jutting peaks, it was not hard to understand how the desert could fortify a people for its task of building a holy nation.

Even in modern Israel, it still is possible to locate Jews who yearn to fulfill their ancient destiny. I discovered them in Hebron, where Abraham had dwelt by the terebinths of Mamre in biblical Kiryat Arba. When Sarah died, he purchased the Machpelah caves for her tomb. In a puzzling departure from Middle Eastern practice (then as now), Abraham insisted upon paying four hundred silver shekels, the full purchase price. Although the land was already promised to him by God, Abraham must have known that without clear legal title he still was a "sojourner," a wanderer. By paying Ephron the Hittite his asking price, Abraham meant to assure that the validity of his foothold in the land could never be challenged.

Hebron always remained a holy city to Jews, but during centuries of Moslem domination they were denied access to the tombs of their patriarchs and matriarchs. Jews were permitted to climb no higher than the seventh step outside the mosque that enclosed the tombs, the mosque itself a vivid symbol of Islamic suppression of Jewish claims. Jewish life in Hebron ended brutally in 1929, when marauding Arabs massacred nearly seventy Jews, mostly yeshiva students. The remainder fled for safety. In 1949, when King Abdullah of Jordan annexed land west of the Jordan river to his kingdom, Hebron was completely closed to Jews. Not until 1967, after Israel's victory in the Six Day War, could they return, first to pray at the tombs and then to rebuild their decimated community in the new settlement of Kiryat Arba overlooking the city.

I retained vivid memories of Hebron from my first trip to Israel, when we sped past Beit Hadassah, the old Jewish medical clinic in the center of town. Inhabited by a tiny cluster of Jewish families, it was an armed fortress. Besieged by Arab hostility, protected by Israeli soldiers, and sustained by the passionate commitment of its residents to God's promise of the land to Abraham's seed, forever, these Jews clung tenaciously to their ancient claims.

To the outside world, and even to many Israelis, they were religious fanatics and inflamed zealots, who needlessly infuriated Arabs, obstructed peace, and made secular Jews intensely uncomfortable with their religious fervor. But I wondered whether they were so very different from the legendary generation of secular Zionists who had zealously resettled land on the old coastal plain of the Philistines, around Rishon LeZion and Tel Aviv.

I felt drawn to the brooding tribal passions, so introverted yet so palpable, in Hebron. But my return was repeatedly frustrated. Once, the town was closed for security reasons; another time, for Ramadan; a mid-winter trip was cancelled by a blizzard. I persevered as though I was not free to stay away. Finally, with the intervention of a friend, I was accompanied to Hebron by Yigal, an army colonel who had been among the first Israeli soldiers to enter the city during the Six Day War. As we drove south from Jerusalem along the road that passes Rachel's tomb to begin a winding ascent into the Hebron hills, a few dozen kilometers became a journey through time.

Yigal and I, virtually the same age, played Jewish geography. We quickly discovered that our paternal grandfathers had been born in Romania. He had not heard of Botosoni, where Jacob lived; nor, he was certain, did I know his grandfather's birthplace. Which village, I politely asked. Piatra Neamt, he replied—where my grandmother Minnie had lived for her first twenty years. It was imaginable that nearly a century earlier our grandparents had played together, as children, in the same Romanian shtetl. Israel, I knew, was like that: the place where Jewish lives intersected, where autobiography and history were fused.

Inside the guarded gates of Kiryat Arba, adjacent to Hebron, ancient claims merged into modern Israel. We drove past the local Bank Leumi and Supersol, along the road that rimmed the settlement. New apartment buildings, tall rectangular blocks faced with stone, jutted incongruously above the weathered landscape. Yet they reminded me of the earliest Jewish neighborhoods in Jerusalem beyond the Old City walls, where houses had turned their backs to the threatening world outside. Here, too, the architectural message was stark: danger is external; inside the enclosure is protected Jewish space.

We visited Rivka, a young Orthodox woman. She described Kiryat Arba as a vastly more comfortable place for Jews than her home town of Louisville. Rivka's living-room walls were book-lined; in a nearby playpen her child was lulled to sleep by a Haydn symphony. Yigal identified a photograph of Rabbi Abraham Isaac Kook, the chief rabbi of Palestine during the Mandatory era and the spiritual mentor of Gush Emunim settlers. In this remote and beleaguered Jewish outpost, I felt surprisingly comfortable. It had an aura of Jewish familiarity. I might have visited my father's relatives in an apartment like this, many years ago.

Our polite conversation was interrupted by the blustery arrival of a man who instantly transformed me into Philip Roth's Eli, the Fanatic, confronting in someone else his own camouflaged Jewish self. Eliezer Waldman, rabbi of the Kiryat Arba yeshiva, was born in Palestine to Czech parents in flight from the Nazis on their way to the United States. He grew up in Williamsburg, leaving Brooklyn to study in a Bnai Akiva yeshiva in Jerusalem. There he met another young rabbinical student, Moshe Levinger. A decade later, their fateful rendezvous at the Park Hotel in Hebron to celebrate Passover ignited the Jewish settlement movement in Judea and Samaria.

I recognized Rabbi Waldman as my Jewish Other, suppressed by Western enlightenment and American freedom. With some reshuffling of history and family circumstance, our life odysseys might have been inverted. When his family fled from the Nazis, mine moved from Philadelphia. While he studied at the Flatbush Yeshiva, I played basketball at Horace Mann. He was a student of Rabbi Tzvi Yehuda Kook in the Mercaz HaRav in Jerusalem while I taught my first American history classes at Brandeis. He encamped in the Park Hotel in Hebron when I bought my first house in a Boston suburb known for its absence of Jews. His fusion of Zionism and Orthodoxy contradicted my synthesis of Judaism and liberalism. While we argued with passionate intensity, I had the unnerving experience of beginning a conversation with another self, my hidden Jewish self.

Struggling to allay my own conflicted feelings, I asked the rabbi to justify his presence in Kiryat Arba. What could he say to diminish the discomfort of American Jews with Jewish settlements on "Arab" land? He rejected my question, for the opinions of American Jews did not concern him. He brusquely dismissed our heightened liberal sensitivities. His agenda was Jewish survival in a Jewish state, within the promised biblical homeland. For the rabbi, settlements were indistinguishable from Israel itself. If Jewish settlement in Hebron was illegitimate, then the legitimacy of Israel, the largest Jewish settlement in the Middle East, also was at risk. Indeed, he continued, if there were illegal Jewish settlements anywhere they could be found in *galut*, in New York and Boston, but certainly not anywhere in the Land of Israel.

I returned to Kiryat Arba a year later, shortly before Rabbi Waldman was elected to the Knesset. Memories of his passionate Jewish intensity lingered. Amid a barrage of election campaign calls, we spoke in his study, at a long table lined with benches for his students. It was an agonizing time in Israel, especially in the settlements. The recent stunning exposure of a Jewish underground and the arrest of some of the most committed Gush Emunim settlers (including his own son-in-law) for violent retaliatory attacks against Arabs raised urgent questions about the morality of Jewish settlement.

The rabbi and I resumed our conversation from the preceding year as though we had merely taken a brief recess. We probed the relation of means to ends, distinctions between Zionist pioneering and hastening the Messianic era, and the meaning of the injunction in Torah not to shed innocent blood. Discussing Jewish ethical obligations, we explored issues of settler culpability, government responsibility, and rabbinical morality. It was an exhilarating intellectual experience in the presence of an extraordinary teacher.

From the rabbi's apartment I went to visit Elyakim Haetzni, a lawyer who had relinquished his successful Tel Aviv practice to live in Kiryat Arba. When I asked why, he explained that he was not a religious man, but he knew that Jewish prayer implored God to return Jews to Zion. He thought it would be a Jewish tragedy if Jews spurned the opportunity. So he had moved.

Arabs in the Land of Israel, Haetzni suggested, were *gerim*, strangers, precisely as the Israelites had been in Egypt. But their lives were as holy as Jewish lives; therefore, they must be protected by law (and he frequently represented Arab clients in Israeli courts). Haetzni vigorously condemned the "religious deviation" of the underground, trying to hasten the arrival of the Messiah with dynamite. We probed the hazy boundary between realistic vision and

messianic fantasy. I noted the contrast between the analytical subtleties and ethical sensitivities that I encountered among the "zealots" of Kiryat Arba and the strident condemnation of settler fanaticism that came so reflexively from my "reasonable" liberal friends.
I was intrigued by the question of whether Zionist Orthodoxy—
the reunification of the religious and national strands of Judaism—
must necessarily erupt into irrational zeal and violence. That spoke
to a far more urgent issue in modern Jewish history: the uneasy
tension between Western secular liberalism and Jewish imperatives. The Jews of Kiryat Arba and Hebron demanded the fidelity
of modern Zionism to the ancient biblical injunction to settle the
promised land. The Torah, not the Enlightenment, was their ultimate source of authority. They never imagined that Moses, who
spoke directly with God, was the precursor of Thomas Jefferson,
speaking for "we the people."

Hebron, even more than Jerusalem, linked Jews to their biblical
patriarchs. The renewed Jewish presence in Hebron was a crucible
for questions about Zionist fidelity to Jewish history. The return of
Jews to their ancient homeland was, after all, what Zionism was all
about. Even Ben-Gurion, the resolutely secular founding father of
Israel, had insisted that the Zionist mandate originated in the Bible.
In Hebron, I drew close to the very source of Jewish civilization in
the Land of Israel.

I respected Jews who still took seriously the covenantal relationship between God, people, and land. They were who I had been
taught not to be. I could easily understand why Hebron Jews were
so profoundly threatening to the Jews of modernity, whether in Tel
Aviv or Harvard Square. Their synthesis of religion and nationality
posed a fundamental Jewish challenge to the fragmentation of
modern Jewish consciousness. Western liberalism's comfortable
distinctions—between knowledge and faith, belief and action, reason and religion—made no sense in Hebron, where Jews lived according to timeless imperatives of Jewish memory and history.

Biblical voices were still audible there, still inspiring tribal faith.
God had told Abraham: "Lift up now thine eyes, and look from the
place where thou art . . . for all the land which thou seest, to thee
will I give it, and to thy seed forever." And Abraham had understood: he moved his tent to "the terebinths of Mamre, which are

in Hebron, and built there an altar unto the Lord." Here Isaac and Ishmael, Abraham's sons, were briefly united to bury their father; here their descendants still live, inextricably bound by their competing claims and mutual hostility.

In Hebron, where past and present converge, I encountered Judaism and Zionism undiluted by modern secularism. My conversation with the Jews who lived there was an extension of my own interior dialogue. I was too much a creature of the American diaspora ever to consider making it my home; but I could not simply dismiss these Jews as aberrant fanatics. I was drawn to them, I knew, because they symbolized the repudiation of all the assimilationist compromises that I had absorbed since childhood.

Israel's invasion of Lebanon in the summer of 1982 provoked a serious rupture between American Jews and the Jewish state. One fundamental justification for this controversial Israeli "war of choice"—to eradicate the Palestinian military state along Israel's northern border—seemed self-evident to me. (Israel's first "war of choice," the 1956 Sinai invasion under Ben-Gurion's leadership, was usually overlooked by Begin's critics.) Demolishing the Palestinian military potential, even for a time short of eternity, was an altogether worthy goal—even if the simultaneous fantasy of Lebanon as a peace partner of Israel could not yet be realized.

The PLO stronghold in south Lebanon, a hotbed of terrorist activity and a vast arsenal of weapons, posed a substantial danger to the security of Israelis in border towns like Kiryat Shemona and Metulla. But those Israelis lived far from Tel Aviv cafés or the faculty lounges on Mt. Scopus, where critics of the invasion gathered to plan their next strategic foray into the *New York Times* or the *New York Review of Books*. I appreciated the reservations of Israelis about war; their sons and husbands would do the fighting and dying. But I was stunned by the venomous response of American Jews, whose only risk was guilt by association, as Jews, with unpopular Israeli policy. For the first time, my allegiance shifted unequivocally from the American diaspora to Israel.

Every morning with breakfast, I encountered a morally delinquent Israel in the *New York Times* (whose enduring Jewish problem was still transmitted through Sulzberger family genes). There were endless editorial variations on what a friend labeled its "Anthony Lewis conjugation": "Israel will lose its soul; Israel is losing its soul; Israel has lost its soul." In a quite remarkable confession, the Reform spokesman Albert Vorspan confided that American Jews were "traumatized" by Israeli behavior. Suffering "shame and stress," they wanted "to crawl into a hole," where they might evade association with the "political and moral bankruptcy" of the Jewish state. American Jews, after all, were "implicated" in Israel's actions: "It's about us."

I, too, felt sickened and implicated. Not by Israel, however, but by the capitulation of American Jews in the face of a barrage of ferocious media criticism of the Jewish state. Its most graphic illustration, for me, came at the level of personal friendship, which I had always naively assumed to be immune to political disagreements. One friend, whose overwrought rendition of his personal conversion in Israel I had patiently endured, quickly reconsidered once Israel was charged with high crimes in the court of public opinion. Quivering with outrage, he abruptly informed me over lunch that my moral defects as a defender of Israel disqualified me from his friendship.

Nor was he alone. Much of what I learned about the early weeks of the Lebanon invasion came from an Israeli who had discovered greener academic pastures in Boston. Back in Israel for a family visit during the summer of the invasion, she had wangled her way across the northern border, as many Israelis did during those first heady days of victory. She returned outraged, brimming with stories of Palestinian perfidy: brave warriors who fired on Israeli soldiers from behind a protective shield of women and children; noble fighters who raised surrender flags only to explode grenades among the Israelis who fell into their trap. Angrily, she denounced American Jews for their hypocrisy in criticizing Israel—until, a month later, she joined the chorus of Israel-bashers. Once again, I was deemed an unworthy friend.

But these were only marginal participants in the flight of Jews from Israel, a spiritual *yerida* (descent) of massive proportions. Internalizing the indictments of Israel's most hostile critics, they imputed moral suicide, even brutal genocide, to Israel. I wondered, instead, whether it was their own failure of nerve I was witnessing.

I thought it likely, as one Israeli observed, that "the only Jews in America frightened by [Israeli] policies are frightened American Jews." When my erstwhile friend conceded that he no longer could draw any moral distinction for his own children between Israeli soldiers and PLO terrorists, I was disgusted.

I was also stunned by the eagerness of American Jewish spokesmen to abandon Israel to protect their own public image in the United States. (That, I knew, was hardly novel: during the Arab riots of 1929, which claimed nearly one hundred Jewish lives, Louis Brandeis, still the revered leader of American Zionists, had privately counseled Jewish silence.) The new editor of the Zionist journal *Midstream*, which had previously published several of my essays, eagerly accepted my critique of American Jewish leaders. After circulating it among their allies he suddenly reconsidered, deciding to publish it only if I sanitized it. American Jews, precisely as Chaim Weizmann had complained after the 1929 riots, still had "cold feet."

In my own quandary as an American Jew, I realized that I no longer could assert, reflexively or unconditionally, that my loyalty was only to the United States. Nor, in the effete way that German Jews had once resolved their loyalty conflict (claiming that they were Jews of the Mosaic persuasion), could I comfortably assert that I was an American whose religion was Judaism. It was not merely a matter of national identity and religious faith, as reassuring as that disjunction might be. I was not a Jewish American, an American who happened to be Jewish; but an American Jew, a Jew who happened to live in the United States. An American citizen, I nonetheless belonged to the Jewish people. Usually, I could balance these attachments. By the fall of 1982, however, the conflict between my country and my people seemed all but irreconcilable.

I tried to resolve my dilemma with a public affirmation of Jewish allegiance, even at the expense of American patriotism. But my published confession, which provoked a lengthy symposium in a Jewish journal, made me feel even more isolated. Milton Konvitz, a legal scholar who once described himself as a "Hellenistic Jew" living comfortably in two worlds, could not even imagine the dilemma that I described. The hyphen between Jewish and American was "a connection" that he cherished, hardly an existential problem. To be a single-minded Jew, he thought, was "a form of monomania" (from which single-minded Hellenistic Jews, presumably, were spared). Philip Klutznick of the World Jewish Congress thought my problem quite simple: I need only "go to Israel forthwith." And Leo Pfeffer, veteran litigator of church-state separation cases for the American Jewish Congress, cited a Hebrew prophet or two, the better to accuse me of "amoral nationalism." I was slightly consoled by writer Anne Roiphe's subtle warning, as she wrestled with her own loyalty dilemma, that "sometimes the chameleon sitting on a leaf thinks he is a leaf. That is a sad illusion."

By then, no longer a Jewish chameleon on an American leaf, I yearned for a different habitat. Another fortuitous invitation from the American Jewish Committee brought me back to Israel in 1984, with yet another group of American Jewish academics. Our assignment was to converse with Israelis about Israel-diaspora relations, severely strained after years of Likud political dominance, Gush Emunim settlement activity, and the Lebanon war.

A dozen years earlier, in my first Israel seminar, I had been the innocent abroad, blithely viewing Israel through my American liberal lenses. Now, however, I felt more like a spy, for the arc of my own interior journey had taken me to places quite remote from the intellectual territory occupied by my American Jewish colleagues. And I knew how little patience Israelis, regardless of their political persuasion, have for the "identity" issues that periodically torture American Jews. Israelis assume that such torments are endemic to *galut*; they prefer to probe the existential drama of Jewish life in the Jewish state.

Just a few days into our seminar, the predictable conflict erupted. An Israeli academic (an Orthodox Jew) had the temerity to reject the reflexive American commitment to the tolerant virtues of ambiguity, complexity, and compromise. He asserted, instead, the validity of "Jewish" imperatives: biblical text, truth, tradition, religious and national distinctiveness. These, he conceded, challenged the liberal democratic values that Americans cherished so deeply. Instantly, he aroused the special fury that liberal intellectuals reserve for those who question their fundamental assumptions. During our time together, Israelis and Americans constantly talked past each other. The refusal of Israelis to affirm the American diaspora experience elicited the counter-claim of the superior moral sensitivity of American Jews. It almost seemed that criticism of Israel had become the primary means of American Jewish self-validation. We could be better Jews, paradoxically, by distancing ourselves with moral outrage from the Jewish state. We had to be reminded, finally, that Jewish identity is rooted in the enduring attachment of the Jewish people to their own homeland. Our instructor, citing the Hebrew Bible as his source, was Father Marcel Dubois, a Maronite Catholic priest who taught philosophy at the Hebrew University. The irony was painful.

Some weeks later, back in Cambridge, memories of these seminar debates were rekindled. In the Harvard congregation I still attended, faithfully but with diminishing enthusiasm, I was invited to comment on the weekly Torah reading. I hesitated, because our Torah discussions often became mired in self-indulgent verbosity (perhaps befitting Harvard academics). But the Korach episode intrigued me. Set in Sinai during the desert wanderings that followed the exodus, it was the climax to a crescendo of "murmurings" against the leadership of Moses. First Miriam and Aaron, speaking against their brother, challenged his direct access to God; Miriam, for her impudence, became leprous. God reminded them that only with Moses did He speak "mouth to mouth." Then the Israelites, fearful after their spies returned from Canaan with reports of the hostile giants who awaited them, turned angrily upon Moses to demand a return to the security of Egypt. Finally, Korach led the rebellion known in Jewish history as "the Great Mutiny."

With several hundred other "princes of the congregation" who were identified as "the elect" of Israel, Korach issued his ostensibly democratic challenge to Moses and Aaron: "You take too much upon you, seeing all the congregation are holy, every one of them, and the Lord is among them; why then do you raise yourselves above the congregation of the Lord." The rabbis, I learned, had dismissed Korach as an ambitious demagogue, a rabble-rouser who seduced his followers with appeals to their gnawing envy of Moses. (After the second-century Bar Kochba revolt was ruthlessly suppressed, the rabbis became exceedingly wary of political challenges to ruling authority.) But the response of Moses, asserting a divine mandate for his leadership, sharpened the issue: what was the ultimate source of Torah, the fundamental law of Israel? Did authority derive from God, as Moses claimed, or, as Korach insisted, must authority be shared by all members of the holy community?

The issue, Moses responded, was for God to decide. If Korach's democratic challenge had merit, he would live out his natural life. If not, God would respond appropriately. The next day, "the earth opened her mouth" and swallowed Korach and his fellow rebels. If there was any lingering doubt about the meaning of the episode, it was resolved in the parallel reading from the first Book of Samuel, where Israel was admonished not to rebel against divine command. In Jewish tradition, divine authority (rabinically interpreted), not *vox populi*, was the only source of legitimacy.

This textual message was no more pleasing to my fellow Harvard congregants than it had been to Korach. Not only did it assert divine authority, a difficult enough principle for an enlightened modern Jew to accept, but it was an explicit textual repudiation of democratic equality. It was not easy, as our testy discussion quickly demonstrated, for American Jews to confront some fundamental incompatibilities between Jewish tradition and American values. To take the Torah text seriously might actually require the recognition that Jewish and American claims occasionally conflicted, even irreconcilably. What then?

Questions like these hovered nearby as I began to plan another sabbatical year in Israel. I was, by then, remarried. Susan, more familiar with Jewish ritual than I had been when we stood together under the *huppa*, was a hesitant participant in my quest. At peace with her own blend of Judaism and American liberalism, she could not fathom my persistent restlessness for Israel. We tacitly agreed to defer consideration of my nagging "Jewish question."

Familiar departure anxieties were accentuated by my father's perceptible decline. Past eighty, wearied by thirty years of travel, he had recently sold his share of his diamond business and gladly retired. But with nothing to do, and my mother's illness unabated, he drifted steadily into apathy. I sensed his fear that he would not live to see me return from Israel, a fear that I secretly shared. I hardly dared to confide to him that not only did I intend the year in Israel for research and writing; I had begun to think of it as a trial preparation for *aliya*.

By then, I looked to my own writing for clues to the subtext of my life. My first book, written in the flush of my New Deal liberalism, had analyzed the struggle for civil liberties during the great labor union organizing drives of the '30s. It displayed my continuing preoccupation with the Roosevelt years, the formative era of my own political consciousness. I had been concerned with liberty, justice, and freedom of speech; there was no room in my life, or my footnotes, for Jews.

Then my old nemesis, the legal profession, engaged me. Writing about lawyers enabled me to express my deepening disillusionment with American society. With a zeal for legal research that I never displayed in law school, I read through forty years of musty bound volumes of obsolete legal periodicals and scanned the letters of more verbose lawyers than I had ever wanted to encounter. Along the way, as I tapped vast professional reservoirs of anti-Semitism, I was astonished to discover my own visceral aversion to it. I would not have cared enough about Jewish issues, I imagined, to become agitated. I had deluded myself. Not only did historical evidence of anti-Semitism distress me, but contemporary excuses for it, sprinkled through some reviews of my book, were infuriating. Judaism, it seemed, mattered to me.

The further I distanced myself from American public life, the easier it became for me to approach Jewish issues less obliquely. In a sequel about justice without law, the perennial American search for alternatives to litigation, I explored patterns of Jewish dispute resolution, carefully devised over time to preserve the rule of Jewish law and insulate Jews from Gentile legal systems. I was searching for my own protected Jewish space at the periphery of American culture.

Now, during some random exploratory reading for my new project, still only vaguely defined, I encountered Yohanan ben Zakkai, the first-century rabbi whose fateful response to the Roman conquest of Jerusalem and destruction of the Second Temple had decisively molded rabbinic Judaism. Relocating to Yavneh, where he elevated study and prayer above political action, he found a way for Judaism to survive and endure once it was deprived of national sovereignty and its cultic center in the Jerusalem Temple. I had stumbled, quite inadvertently, upon a profoundly consequential moment in Jewish history, the emergence of rabbinical legal authority.

As I began to pair lawyers, whose sphere of (American) authority I had finally rejected, with rabbis, whose (Jewish) religious authority I had barely encountered, I reached an odd convergence of autobiography and history. For most modern Jews, rabbinical legal authority was an obsolete relic of the dark ages of Jewish history. Yet there I was, traveling backward in time, substituting rabbis for lawyers, relinquishing American acculturation for Jewish identification.

Some quirky coincidences during the final month before my departure to Israel reinforced my sense of being swept along by irresistible currents of personal destiny. Previous journeys to Israel should have prepared me. My vintage experience was an adventure with my first Jerusalem souvenir, a beret that I had purchased in a Ben Yehuda Street hat store. It was my talisman, which accompanied me whenever I returned to Israel. But many trips later, on my last morning in Jerusalem, I could not find it anywhere. Frantic, I raced downtown to the same store, only to learn that it no longer stocked berets. "Where?" I implored, depleting my Hebrew vocabulary almost by half. The owner gestured across the street.

But his neighbor shrugged, and sent me off to Hamashbir, the department store around the corner. Several salesmen in the hat department, with nothing better to do that morning, convened to discuss my plight. Finally, one of them drew a map on a piece of scrap paper for the next stage of my treasure hunt. I crossed Jaffa Road, pushed my way through throngs of Friday shoppers, to the Geula neighborhood abutting Mea Shearim. There I finally located Resnick's hat store, where the saleswoman reassured me that she had exactly what I wanted. Indeed, she admonished me, I should have known enough to come there first.

Thanking her profusely, I detoured to Mea Shearim to say goodbye to a friend; then, with time for wandering, I explored some unfamiliar side streets. Turning a corner, I stopped to watch a frail old woman vigorously beat her carpets, a venerable pre-Sabbath ritual. Young girls, with sparkling eyes and long braids, hugged challahs on their way home. Hasidic men scurried by, hastening to conclude the week's business. In the midst of an Orthodox shtetl, I glanced at the nearby street sign to locate myself. I was standing at the corner of Rehov Efraim Auerbuch, named in honor of the nineteenth-century chief rabbi of Jerusalem.

Late the next night, at Ben-Gurion airport, I reached passport control with the dismaying realization that while my new beret was safely packed, now my passport was missing. As I retraced my steps to the ticket counter, I heard my name on the public address loudspeaker. As I stepped off the escalator, a security guard handed me my passport. "Perhaps," he suggested with a wry smile, "you do not wish to leave."

Acquainted with these travel gremlins, I was not entirely surprised to learn the identity of our new street address in Jerusalem. It was named (HaTibonim) for a pair of brothers, both rabbis, who were known for their interpretation of Maimonides' *Guide to the Perplexed*, the brilliant medieval attempt to reconcile reason and faith. An appropriate location for me, I reflected. Browsing in a local bookstore, I found a book about the Western Wall. Scanning the notes, I discovered a reference to an article in the *Encyclopedia Judaica*, written by one J. Auerbach. Curious, I checked: my namesake, appropriately, was identified only as "Jacob Auerbach, Jerusalem"—precisely who I was about to become.

A final coincidence: on my forty-ninth birthday, I gave my farewell Torah talk at Harvard. I vaguely recalled the weekly reading, *Behar*, from my own bar mitzvah. I had next encountered it thirty years later, for my son's bar mitzvah. Now I finally read it carefully. *Behar* completes the cycle of Sabbaths. The seventh day is mandated as a day of rest for people; the seventh year is a time of "solemn rest for the land," when tilling, reaping and sowing were prohibited. *Behar* instructs that after seven seven-year cycles, on Yom Kippur of the forty-ninth year, the *shofar* is blown to proclaim a Jubilee year. The Jubilee was a holy year when the entire community of Israel—people, land, nation—was expected to turn away from mundane necessities to experience spiritual and moral elevation. All landed property would revert back to its original owners and Hebrew slaves would be freed. Recurring at forty-nine year intervals, a Jubilee might be experienced only once in a lifetime.

As my own Jubilee year began, I felt the power of the ancient biblical summons "to hallow the fiftieth year."

My favorite Jerusalem bus, the number 9, circumnavigates the city. Like a wayward explorer, it winds its way from sedate Rehavia through a tumultuous downtown crossing near Zion Square; then it skirts the edge of Orthodox Mea Shearim and cuts through the Sephardic Bukharin Quarter; released from the bends and angles of narrow old streets, it hurtles past the stark new apartment towers of Ramot Eshkol and dips briefly into Arab east Jerusalem before beginning its final ascent to the university heights astride Mt. Scopus. During my early weeks back in Jerusalem I often rode this bus, zig-zagging through the city in an endless round of errands and appointments. I yearned for different journeys, but I was still confused about my route and uncertain of my destination.

The frenzy of adjustment was heightened by the imminence of Rosh ha-Shanah. Eager for familiar melodies and the comfort of ritual, I searched for a compatible synagogue. But my efforts veered from comedy to farce. The synogogue I knew best (but, of course, rarely attended) had relocated so far away that it would have taken the better part of the holiday morning to push our stroller there— as I discovered after an exhausting evening trudging up and down the hills of Kiryat Shmuel and San Simon in an attempt to locate it. At the venerable Conservative synagogue nearby, I was offered seats so far from the *bima* that we were almost across the street in Independence Park. I tried the campus of the Jewish Theological Seminary, only to be told that its synagogue was closed for the holy days!

Thwarted, I chose serendipity. Just before the sundown of Rosh ha-Shanah, I turned our corner to Azza Road, normally teeming with traffic but now startlingly quiet in the late afternoon shadows. An old man, resplendent in his white *kittel* and fur hat, trudged slowly up the hill. A father whose three children scrambled to keep pace raced by. I followed them to my unknown destination as the sirens that proclaim holy time in Jerusalem echoed throughout the city.

As I entered the synogogue, mild anxiety erupted into surging panic. It was instantly obvious that I had stumbled into a Hasidic *shul.* I heard Yiddish everywhere, but little Hebrew and no English. Conspicuous in my short-sleeved white shirt, I was the only man not enclosed in black. Too paralyzed to leave, I felt myself spinning back to my childhood, the week before my bar mitzvah, when I was surrounded by old Jewish men and imprisoned in Jewish space and time.

I asked—of no one in particular—"Is it all right for me to be here?" A heavily accented English voice responded, almost kindly, "Where is it better for you to be tonight?" I was comforted, slightly. Suddenly, without any discernible signal, a pounding for silence triggered the wordless chant that precedes the call to prayer. Resounding through the small building, the pronouncement of the days of awe and judgment echoed deep inside me.

Later, at dinner with our new neighbors, Moshe smiled when I recounted my travail. "You should have come upstairs," he gently admonished me. There I might have felt less intimidated in his minyan of *mitnagdim*, the historical opponents of the emotional and spiritually relentless *hasidim*. How, I wondered, could I have intuited this synagogue version of upstairs-downstairs?

The next day, at a pallid service mostly attended by transplanted Americans, I was no more comfortable. I felt oppressed by the polite decorum, annoyed by a liturgy altered to reflect discomfort with references to God or Jewish distinctiveness, and irritated by a litany of appeals on behalf of worthy liberal causes. If the Eastern European shtetl was not my spiritual world, neither was a blend of temperate Judaism and inflamed morality transplanted from the Upper West Side of Manhattan.

For several weeks, as holy days came and went, I persisted in my quest for a congenial synagogue. The alternatives preferred by secular Israelis, the beaches of Tel Aviv or a holiday abroad, had no appeal. But since I did not know what I wanted or precisely why I wanted it, it was hardly surprising that I could not find it. Even in Jerusalem, I was still a wandering Jew.

Reflecting my spiritual malaise, my body suddenly responded with two days of acute physical discomfort. The anxiety of an undiagnosed illness was heightened by the absence of familiar comforts such as my own physician, instant pharmacy service, and hot bath water. With uncanny timing, the crisis peaked on a *Shabbat* morning when medical services were available only in the emergency room of the duty hospital in a remote precinct of the city. In desperation, Susan telephoned the home of the chief urologist at Hadassah hospital, with whom I had an appointment scheduled for the following week. His wife revealed the telephone code that would alert him, upon his return from synagogue, to my urgent need. Rather than send me to the nearest emergency room, his most convenient option, the doctor immediately summoned me to his home office. There, with consummate tenderness, he eased my agony, wrote out a prescription for antibiotics, and assured me that all would be well.

Afterward, we stood together on the steps of his elegant Talbieh house. This small, bearded pixie of a man, his jacket now carefully rebuttoned and his *Shabbat* serenity restored, insisted that if, "God forbid," I needed him again, I must not hesitate to telephone. Then a taxi, which his wife had called in yet another merciful breach of Sabbath observance, arrived to take us home. With physical health restored, my spirits soared and the fever of my misery was broken. I tried to relax my expectations and to accept my destiny as an outsider in two countries: uncomfortably Jewish in the United States, conspicuously American in Israel.

Heartened by my newly discovered equanimity, I set off for Haifa to bring our trunks through customs. Among the various ordeals that Israelis have devised to demonstrate how precarious sanity truly is in a Jewish state, customs inspection ranks high. Despite the advice of knowledgeable friends (which we had faithfully followed), the inspector fixated upon my manual typewriter (fifteen years old), an electric traveling iron (worth five dollars), and a short-wave cassette radio (our only material indulgence) as the last best hope to rectify Israel's trade deficit. He set duty charges that more than doubled the listed purchase prices of our items. When I asked my shipping agent for advice, he laconically responded that I might contest the charges.

By then, however, the customs official had lowered his window shade for *hafsaka*, the predictable interlude in the Israeli work day that assured enfeebled productivity. When, precisely fifteen minutes later, he snapped up the shade, I lost control. I screamed my intention to repack my trunks on the spot, returning anything that might incur even a single shekel of duty charges. He shrugged indifferently, but I noticed that he had begun to recalculate so I shouted still louder. He quickly reached the precise figure, lower by two-thirds, that my agent had predicted. We exchanged polite smiles, and I yielded my place to the next contestant in this Levantine sport. I savored my triumph for, at the mere risk of a coronary embolism, I had bargained successfully. I thought that I might yet become comfortable in Israel.

Trying to learn Hebrew quickly disabused me of the notion. Ever since junior high school, I had been hopelessly inept in foreign languages. I barely survived Spanish, and the graduate-school ordeal of a reading exam in French almost deprived me of my doctorate. Hebrew had different, but no less painful, associations. If I had even learned the aleph-bet in Hebrew school, I had long since forgotten it.

My Jerusalem ulpan certainly attracted a more fascinating cast of characters than Hebrew school ever had. In my introductory class, the two largest student clusters were Jerusalem Arabs preparing for jobs in local banks or municipal offices and a coterie of French Jesuits on study leave to add modern Hebrew to their array of biblical languages. I was seriously disadvantaged, for I had neither the familiarity with Semitic languages nor the passion for homework that propelled my classmates to fluency.

After twenty years of teaching, it was painful to become a beginning student once again. Worse yet, as someone for whom linguistic precision was everything, I felt hopelessly preliterate. Before too long, I functioned as the class dunce, rivaled only by Menachem, a tiny gnome of a man who had survived a Polish concentration camp and finally reached Israel after thirty years in Argentina. He charmed us with twenty words in at least a dozen languages, but he never managed to arrange any of them in a complete sentence.

Our teacher, Ruth, with deft skill and remarkable patience, translated our most halting and meager efforts into coherence. But the more captivating her efforts, the more rapidly I regressed. A little boy once again, I listened raptly to her spare yet magically compelling biblical stories and historical narratives, recounted in a simple Hebrew that, to my astonishment, even I could comprehend. I was as excited as our two-year-old daughter Shira, just then mastering the fundamentals of language as she indiscriminately mixed the English she heard at home with the Hebrew she learned in *gan*. At her bedtime, I retold Ruth's stories and composed simple Hebrew rhymes. One night, I even awoke from a dream in Hebrew. As long as I could speak in the present tense and evade hazardous rules of conjugation, I enjoyed myself. But grammatical complexities increased, along with the drudgery of vocabulary memorization. As my frustration mounted, I channeled my resentment toward Ruth's alternate, a ruthless drillmaster whose forced marches through irregular verbs were excruciating. After three months, simultaneously assaulted by the past and future tenses, I feared that the entire year would become hostage to my Hebrew ineptitude.

Instead, I resumed my Jerusalem wanderings. Perhaps a face, an arch, a gate, a gnarled olive tree, at the intersection of Jewish history and personal memory, might begin to unravel the timeless mysteries of that holy city. I listened for a whisper of a clue why Jews, ever since the Babylonian exile, could never forget Jerusalem—and whether, finally, I belonged among them.

My point of departure was Talbieh or Rehavia, the neighborhoods I had lived in and knew best. Old Talbieh, once a tiny enclave outside the Old City for wealthy Arab and Armenian Christians and foreign diplomats, displays the most beautiful houses in Jerusalem. Built during the World War I era, their arches, domes, recessed balconies, and painted tiles evoke a bygone epoch of Christian ascendancy and colonial empire. Along Hovevei Zion, sedate old stone houses with majestic arched windows framed in blue tile borders overlooking lush gardens offer serene refuge from the tribal animosities that fester elsewhere in Jerusalem. It is my favorite street in the entire city.

Rehavia, once a garden suburb for German refugees from Hitler, remains more middle European than middle Eastern. Along its shaded streets—Ben Maimon, Rashba, Alfasi—chamber music often floats from the old stone houses that are wrapped in veils of flowering vines. In an elongated park across Ramban Street, near where I once lived, I could recall a moment of humiliation from my first year in Jerusalem. After taking Jeff and Pammy to school, I usually returned this way, choosing a favorite bench for reading the daily newspapers. Most mornings, a husky man walked his enormous dog past me, occasionally unleashing him for a run. Once, after a sharp command, the dog instantly obeyed. Even the dog, I conceded sadly, knew more Hebrew than I did.

Across from the high school entrance, where clusters of youngsters flirted throughout the day (while their teachers enjoyed *hafsaka*), I detoured to a nearby stationery store for the Jerusalem *Post*. I marveled at the diabolical cleverness of the owner, a lanky longbearded man shuffling about in slippers, who frequently rearranged his counters to create an ever-more maddening bottleneck at the front door. A few steps away, at Edit's bakery, I stopped for coffee. Her cinnamon-raisin danish was irresistible, and from an outside table I could watch the morning pedestrian flow, as late workers scurried past early shoppers. Across the street was the post office where I had first encountered my cousin whom I had not seen in twenty-five years. On the next corner, Yitzhak from Iraq sold old copper pitchers and bowls. It was my neighborhood.

From there, I roamed through the nearby shtetl of Shaaray Hesed (Gates of Righteousness), one of the first Jewish neighborhoods built outside the Old City. An old-world enclave, it is overshadowed at its western edge by the towering skyscrapers of Kiryat Wolfson, a modern architectural monument to tasteless wealth. But Shaaray Hesed remains a beguiling walled city-within-a-city; the original enclosure, broken only by a single gate, still forms its northern boundary. Many of its houses, too flimsy with age to stand alone, lean inward upon each other, connected by rickety stairs and braced with tin annexes.

A large synagogue with an intricate sundial on one exterior wall dominates the neighborhood. The murmur of prayer is always audible. I often stopped nearby, perching on an old cistern to listen to the rhythmic hum from within. The old men, white-bearded and black-coated, might just have arrived from the nineteenth century. Once I walked through Shaaray Hesed during a bitter cold Chanukah night. Flames flickered outside every doorway from the glass-enclosed Jerusalem *hanukiot* that shield burning wicks against the winter wind and rain. I returned to Shaaray Hesed in all seasons, to absorb the distinctive sounds and rhythms of the shtetl.

From Shaaray Hesed, I skirted the downtown edge of the city until I reached Mahane Yehuda, the market neighborhood that is the belly of Jerusalem. A crowded warren of decrepit old houses, squeezing each other along narrow alleys barely wide enough for a car and person to pass simultaneously, it is home to working-class Sephardic Jews from North Africa and the Middle East. By the time I came by, the neighborhood children already were in school, the men were at work in their market stalls, and the women were returning home with their bulging shopping sacks, or washing floors and hanging laundry outside.

The southern edge of the market is Rehov Agrippas, lined with cheap clothing and food stores, a restaurant-grill serving "bifstek" and "cheeps" at every corner. It is the gateway to tumult. Inside the tin-roofed arcades of the market, shoppers jostle for space and bargains, adeptly using their parcels as battering-rams to clear a path. Behind pyramids of fruit and vegetables (woe to the shopper who does not prefer the tomatoes at the top), sellers with stentorian voices boom their wares, flinging produce on and off their scales too quickly for me (or, perhaps, anyone) to receive an accurate reading. I seldom shopped in the *shuk*, but it offers the best street theatre in town.

I went there for the people, not the produce. In its murky passageways, sound and motion merge in a seething sea of human variety: Hasidic men, Bedouin women, Armenian priests, Ethiopian monks, Jews from everywhere between the Atlas Mountains and Vilna, women wearing babushkas and men in tattered jackets and baggy pants, Arabs in flowing robes, Israeli soldiers on patrol. If I timed my visit for lunch, I found a table in my favorite hummus restaurant, a perfect spectator perch overlooking the busiest intersection of the market.

Once I sat next to a solitary, dignified, old Arab man, just finishing his midday meal. Because the *shuk*, especially on Fridays, is packed with people, it has occasionally been the preferred site for a terrorist's pipe-bomb. I made certain that my companion's shopping bag, wedged under the table, accompanied him when he departed. I would like to be more tolerant, but I have been socialized by Middle-Eastern realities.

The Sephardic working-class exuberance of Mahane Yehuda, raw and vocal, offers startling Jewish counterpoint to Rehavia civility and Shaaray Hesed insularity. Here, rage and love and every emotion in between are openly, loudly, and continuously on display. During the election campaigns of the 1980s, the political heroes of the *shuk*, Menachem Begin and Ariel Sharon, were ecstatically hailed as "Melech Israel"— King of Israel. I have no friends here, and I have little in common with these Jews of the *shuk*. But we are all Jews nonetheless, and the strange mixture of our common heritage and vast disparities fascinates me.

Ever since I wandered into Mea Shearim during my first visit to Jerusalem, I felt its discomforting allure. The oldest, largest Hasidic enclave in the city, it is the reincarnation of Poland in the nineteenth, or perhaps seventeenth, century. Its gates open into another world, the vanished world of Eastern European Orthodoxy. Mea Shearim, enclosed by Jewish law and tribal folkways, is intensely suspicious of outsiders. Here, glances communicate more than words: eyes twinkle at friends, or flicker at strangers; men and women ostentatiously avert their eyes from each other; children's eyes shine with innocent curiosity; adult eyes burn with zealous intensity, whether for God or business profit it is impossible to know.

I never yearned, or learned, to penetrate the sectarian mysteries of Mea Shearim, whose origins lie in venerable rabbinical dynasties. I could not distinguish a Satmar from a Belzer, or either from Naturei Karta, the anti-Zionist zealots who deny the very legitimacy of a Jewish state and have occasionally entreated Yasir Arafat to terminate its existence. The intricacies of their piety and politics intrigue me less than the insularity of their world from the contagious and subversive enticements of modernity. Here is Jewish life before emancipation, retaining its own secrets about the stubborn tenacity that enabled Judaism to survive the worst that the Christian West could inflict upon it.

This remnant of Eastern European Orthodoxy, the "black hats" as they are contemptuously labeled by secular Israelis, has been described with a mixture of disdain and apprehension. "The incredible vitality of this Judaism," the popular novelist Amos Oz wrote despairingly, "threatens your own spiritual existence and eats away at the roots of your own world." Worse yet, this Orthodoxy—"eternally unchanged . . . forever stagnant"—nonetheless flourishes in the very Zionist state that was intended to replace it. To secular zealots like Oz (and my enlightened Israeli friends), Mea Shearim is nothing but a vestigial island of religious fanaticism, the living demonstration of its own obsolescence in a rational world.

Mea Shearim never threatened my spiritual existence. Instead, it evoked a past that I never knew I had until it was too late to recapture it. As a stranger, in the various disguises of modernity, I was hardly noticed there. Among the old men of Mea Shearim, I often saw my grandfather Jacob or heard whispered echoes of his voice. Its store windows, filled with religious articles, reminded me of the Lower East Side, where my father had taken me for my bar mitzvah *tallit*. I wandered aimlessly down narrow alleys, into the courtyards where neighborhood life pulsated with activity, in and out of stores, until my invisibility finally became oppressive. Then, drawn by the high-pitched cadences of young boys enthusiastically reciting their lessons and prayers, I headed for the yeshiva building that faces the main square of the neighborhood.

There, in a nondescript corner store with dusty, empty windows, I had discovered David Ezra. When I first wandered into his store, I was certain that I had made a foolish mistake. David, a gruff and husky man, was seated in a corner, surrounded by empty shelves. I sat down on a rickety wooden chair, and waited. Commanding me to join him for coffee, David swiveled awkwardly in his chair, flicked on an electric burner, reached for cups, mixed ingredients from jars and packets, and poured the most delicious brew I had ever tasted. Then we began to talk in a conversation punctuated by long interruptions that has lasted for twenty years.

Several generations ago, David's family came to Jerusalem from Baghdad. Like his father before him, in the same store, David sells old copper pitchers, bowls, jugs, and trays brought by immigrants from the Bukharan region of Persia, Uzbekistan, and elsewhere in the Middle East. Sooner or later, when they need money, they come to David to sell. I quickly came to appreciate David's knowledge and relish his stories. He taught me to feel copper for weight and to identify the delicately engraved, highly stylized patterns. I was fortunate to learn, from someone else's costly mistake in my presence, never—ever—to bargain with David. His price, after all, was fair! Any challenge to his authority transformed David into a wrathful demon. Breathing heavily, rolling his dark expressive eyes, deepening his voice, he banished the offender from his store, forever. And David never forgot a face.

Among my various treasures from David—including a splendid water jug and assorted pitchers as delicately tapered as minarets—I especially cherished a pair of Warsaw candlesticks. David anticipated my silent fantasy and instantly quashed it, informing me that they probably had accompanied Polish Jews during the third *aliya*, after World War I. But with "Warsawa" clearly stamped inside the base, their provenance was indisputable.

Months later I asked an American friend, whose parents had emigrated from Warsaw, to inquire whether his mother recognized the manufacturer's name. He telephoned back to tell me how my innocent request had detonated within his family. No sooner had he posed my question to his mother, in the presence of her sister, than the two women erupted in bitter recriminations. All the family silver (and, it seemed, the silver of every Jewish family in Warsaw) had been purchased from that very manufacturer. Its "unfair" distribution when the family emigrated still rankled after fifty years.

In time, I visited David to talk, not to buy—although the excitement of possessing yet another intricately engraved pitcher or bowl never receded. A damaged leg limited his mobility, so everyone came to him. To his endless parade of visitors—Hasidim wanting to change money, family members with a problem (ten children kept David busy), his Moroccan friend "Shmuli" from across the street, a Hadassah surgeon who collected old *hanukiot*—David dispensed advice and admonitions. His deep voice thundered pronouncements about Israeli politics, world affairs, American Jews, or child-rearing with the power of ocean waves breaking against a rocky shore. David could say the most outrageous things, and often did, while remaining altogether impervious to disagreement. Whether the issue was Arab terror or unruly children, his solution, as far as I could tell, never varied. David demanded compliance with authority.

An autocratic patriarch, David instructed his wife to prepare a meal for ten guests as easily as he dispatched his nineteen-year-old daughter to her room for switching television channels without his permission. Omnipotent ruler over his business domain, he had no qualms about preventing a customer from buying or expelling him for perceived insults. Suffering a serious heart attack, he refused hospitalization; he continues to drink *arak* with impunity. These are inconsequential flurries in the life of someone who once belonged to the Irgun underground, who was twice imprisoned by the British, and once betrayed by two of his own partners on their way to kill a double agent. David, after all, is a force of nature, and he knows it.

Once, I left David's store to encounter hundreds of Hasidic men, packed silently together on the main street of Mea Shearim. I looked for signs of an accident or a disturbance, but there were none. They waited, so I paused; when they moved, I scurried alongside, trying to detect some clue to their mission. The closer I came to the head of the pack, the more dense it was—a mass of bodies, black and silent. In the crowded center, I finally spotted half a dozen men, each with one arm extended, a hand touching the shoulder of the man in front. Bearing a shrouded corpse, they carried it within this most intimate final enclosure of the living. The funeral procession started and stopped like a single organism, moving silently toward the ancient Jewish cemetery on the Mount of Olives. Transfixed, I felt the power of ritual and respect, community and continuity.

As drawn as I was to the European shtetls of Jerusalem, to neighborhoods inhabited by my Jewish Other, the Old City never lost its fascination. Long after I no longer was a gawking tourist there, I remained an inquisitive explorer. Along the soaring walls of Suleiman, in the subterranean depths of Second Temple ruins, or immersed in the swirling eddies of life in each of its four quarters, I knew my way better than in any neighborhood where I had ever lived.

In the Moslem Quarter, I relinquished my Western sense of

time to comply with leisurely Middle Eastern rhythms. There, I encountered a different "Other"—always intriguing, occasionally menacing, and ultimately elusive. My journey began along a quiet stretch of the Via Dolorosa, inside the Lion's Gate, where I discovered Mahmoud's antiquities shop. Mahmoud, handsome and austere, was the first Arab to study archeology at the Hebrew University after the Six Day War. Once we realized that my Jerusalem cousin was a frequent customer, he mellowed until, over time, we developed a genuine friendship (within the boundaries that he demarcated).

At the rear of his store, away from the wooden camels and crucifixes sold by his brother to passing pilgrims, he instructed me in the historical and archeological intricacies of his trade. Under his tutelage, I learned to distinguish Bronze from Iron Age juglets, Hellenistic from Roman oil lamps, and varieties of Second Temple coins from each other. While my daughter Pammy meticulously arranged his horde of ancient beads by size and color, I explored the astarte fertility figurines in his remarkable collection, sipping coffee while I furtively watched him buy and sell.

One day Mahmoud showed me two tiny perfume juglets, recently excavated from a tomb in Samaria. They were barely an inch tall, each with a deep red patina. One was round and squat; the other slim and tapered; each had a delicate handle; both were perfectly intact. I agonized over which one to buy, for they were not inexpensive. Finally I chose, as delighted with my new treasure as I was disappointed to relinquish its companion.

But I felt vaguely uneasy all that evening and the next day, which I spent hiking in the Judean wilderness. Midway through the afternoon, impulsively, I returned to Mahmoud's store. Mahmoud was startled by my sudden, slightly disheveled appearance. I blurted out my discomfort that I had separated the twin juglets, buried together for two thousand years. Surely they should remain paired; would he now sell me the one I had left behind? To my consternation, Mahmoud's welcoming smile receded into a tight frown. How had I blundered? Mahmoud explained with careful precision, as though he was instructing me in a fine point of archeological etiquette, that he had intended to bring the other juglet home for his own collection; once there, he would not have re-

turned it. But he had inadvertently left it behind in the store overnight. Therefore, he would sell it to me. I appreciated his under-
standing of my craving, which was what we most shared in common.

Like any number of Israelis for whom archaeology is a consum-
ing national and personal passion, I valued each addition to my
small collection as though I had excavated a remnant of my own
past. With indiscriminate eagerness, I gathered oil lamps whose
origins spanned the Hasmonean and Byzantine periods; sturdy red
and black vases and delicate juglets, some dating back beyond the
first Jewish Commonwealth to the patriarchal era; and Canaanite
fertility figures, distinctive with their protruding round eyes,
which predated the arrival of the Israelites from Egypt. Inanimate
though they were, my new companions eloquently evoked the ancient history of the people to whom I now felt intimately linked.

Mahmoud was exceedingly gracious, far beyond the normally
expansive boundaries of Arab hospitality. Often I accompanied
him on his Old City shopping rounds. Occasionally, we might
lunch together in East Jerusalem restaurants where I was the solitary Westerner—and Jew; and once he invited Susan and me to
his home, where he proudly guided us through his magnificent
private collection of antiquities and, from his rooftop, showed us
the lights of Amman twinkling in the distance. But as though by
tacit consent, Mahmoud and I never discussed the most striking
incongruity of our friendship: a Palestinian Arab sharing his archeological knowledge with a diaspora Jew whose attachment to
Israel, he surely knew, deepened with every purchase.

Another of Mahmoud's frequent visitors, with an obsessive passion for collecting antiquities matched only by his apparently limitless resources for acquiring them, was Father Godfrey. A corpu-
lent monk who lived in a tiny cell in Terra Sancta, he had virtually
entombed himself among cartons filled with ancient pottery. Father Godfrey seemed to know about new discoveries almost before
they were dug. He would lumber into Mahmoud's shop, heaving
and perspiring in his brown habit, and whisper conspiratorially.
Then he and Mahmoud raced off together (once I tagged along) to
examine comparable pieces in a private museum nearby in the
Church of the Flagellation, where they enjoyed privileged access. I

appreciated Father Godrey's compulsion, for I came to share it. I happened to stop by the store one day, just after Mahmoud had returned with a gold Roman earring, discovered an hour earlier during nearby street repairs. It was irresistibly beautiful and I bought it immediately for Susan.

A few hundred meters along the Via Dolorosa, in a tiny, dank hole in the wall, sat Ibrahim, a thin wisp of a man whose effusive greeting had once drawn me inside. Everyone was welcome in his store, which could barely accommodate four people comfortably. Ibrahim had managed to ingratiate himself with every ruling authority in modern Jerusalem, from the British through the Jordanians to the Israelis. Easily distracted from his perpetual game of *sheshbesh* with an Arab friend, he flirted shamelessly with young female tourists, negotiated skillfully with knowledgeable Israeli collectors, and haggled relentlessly with Bedouin diggers for their newest treasures, all the while entertaining his appreciative audience.

For reasons that were never apparent, for I was hardly a major customer, Ibrahim went out of his way to guide Susan, Shira, and me to places where we never would have ventured on our own. At the whisper of a hint, he gladly closed his store for an afternoon to drive to the old casbah in Shechem (Nablus), to visit the Samaritan high priest in his ancient synagogue on nearby Mt. Gerezim, to explore the Machpelah tombs in Hebron (where he had participated in Kathleen Kenyon's excavations), to pick oranges from the lush grove of a Jericho friend, or to admire some hand-embroidered dresses by old Arab women in Beit Jalla. Every expedition concluded with a lavish feast at an outdoor restaurant in Ramallah or Jericho, or beneath the grape arbor of his Silwan home.

I trusted Ibrahim, often placing my family in his care in Arab towns and *shuks* where no Jews other than armed Israeli soldiers ventured. But I could never stop wondering whether, in the event of trouble, Ibrahim or Mahmoud would protect me. I often rehearsed the scenario: a sudden stabbing, a shower of stones, an outburst of Arab fury. None of these episodes were unknown in the Old City. If I needed a place of refuge, would I be as welcome in their stores as I had been in their homes? Or would I be abandoned? I never had occasion to learn the answer, but the incongruity of our attachment, with Jewish antiquities as our connecting links, meant that I never could stop asking the question.

Even before the *intifada* virtually closed Arab neighborhoods to Jews, I found myself drifting more comfortably into the Jewish Quarter. As the initial attraction of opposites subsided, the comforts of tribal solidarity deepened. I discovered Jewish counterparts for Mahmoud and Ibrahim. There was an antiquities dealer whose inventory, I suspected, expanded during intelligence missions to Iran. And a map dealer, a wealthy Orthodox Jew from Antwerp, who was astonished that I actually knew the location of the Old City scenes depicted in his nineteenth-century lithographs by Roberts and Bartlett. One afternoon, to test my veracity, he closed his store and, print in hand, followed me to the magnificent fountain, five minutes away, that Bartlett had drawn a century and a half earlier. For the pleasure of our outing, he sold it to me at a substantial discount.

My explorations into Jerusalem space were accompanied by evocative reminders of Jewish time. Early every Friday morning, preceding *Shabbat,* the city pulsated with a final burst of manic energy before it subsided in the gentle sigh of the seventh day. Late in the afternoon, as the sun began to set over the Israel Museum, Shira and I would walk along the rim of the valley overlooking the Monastery of the Cross. There, we claimed our own "secret bench," in a nook enclosed by fragrant shrubs. We chattered together, watching tiny lizards scurry along the stone walls and listening to the chorus of birds singing overhead. Before the *Shabbat* siren rose and fell through the city, I sensed its imminence and we returned home for candle-lighting.

When we were alone, we often overheard our neighbor Yitzhak, across the hall, recite kiddush· and lead his guests in song. Those evenings, I realized sadly, Judaism still came to me through walls. The best Friday nights were with Moshe and Chava, our friends downstairs, who adopted us for the year. They each had endured wracking childhood odysseys that would defy belief were they not the norm among Holocaust survivors of their generation. Moshe, one year old when the Nazis invaded Poland, spent the war years behind Soviet lines in Uzbekistan. There he lost two brothers, one of whom was trying desperately to rejoin their father, stranded in

Palestine after war broke out. Chava lived in Budapest until 1944, when the Nazi roundup in Hungary began. Her grandfather managed to secure places for the entire family on the notorious Kastner train, the only safe exit for Hungarian Jews. After a six-month detour in Bergen-Belsen, while the price of their escape was renegotiated, they continued to Spain and, finally, to Palestine.

On Friday evenings, after returning from synagogue, Moshe presided, firmly but gently. Occasionally he drifted away in fatigue, or memory, but he quickly roused himself to rejoin us. The older boys relaxed from the rigors of army service or yeshiva study; their sister shyly responded to us in English while assertively answering Moshe's probing questions about the weekly Torah reading in Hebrew. Moshe's intense seriousness was moderated by Chava's expansive warmth. Chava was there for everyone, preparing and serving a bountiful dinner and spiritedly singing favorite *Shabbat* melodies.

Everyone sang together, blending their own distinctive family harmonies in song. One vibrant hymn of thanksgiving burrowed so deeply into Shira's musicial memory that long after she had forgotten everything else about Jerusalem, she could still sing it perfectly. I envied Moshe and Chava's seemless fusion of Zionism and Orthodoxy. Their lives embraced the most enduring commands in Jewish history: to dwell in the Land and obey the Law.

Other Israelis, often total strangers, also made me feel that I belonged to their family. There was the Orthodox doctor who had treated me on *Shabbat*. And the telephone operator who persistently called neighbors in my friend's apartment building in Kfar Saba, when his phone was not working, to locate someone who could convey an important message. And the El Al office manager who patiently heard my request to meet Susan, then pregnant, inside the airport baggage terminal, where (for security reasons) only passengers were permitted. Lacking the authority to grant my wish, she nonetheless offered me a ride to Ben-Gurion airport, at 4 A.M. the next morning, so that she could personally present my request to security officers.

As these experiences multiplied, my attachment deepened. I felt it in various ways, but never more strongly than when I crossed the Rafiah border on my return from two weeks in Sinai and Egypt.

Safely beyond the Byzantine intricacies of Egyptian customs, I raced through the neutral zone toward the Israeli flag, fluttering a hundred meters away. As I chatted with a young Sephardic soldier, listening to the staccato bursts of Hebrew on his walkie-talkie, I knew that I was home.

As if reality existed to confirm my fantasies, I returned to Jerusalem to discover that a foundation fellowship assured yet another year in Israel. That might lead to another, and another, until . . . ? I had hardly floated that vision when an even more enticing prospect materialized: an invitation to join the Hebrew University faculty. It was, indisputably, a moment of decision on which the rest of my life would turn.

If anything is more tormenting than denial of a cherished wish, I knew it might be fulfillment. The ironies were painfully evident. At Wellesley, I had persuaded my colleagues that I should offer a course on American Jewish history, although it clearly was outside the boundaries of my professional training. And I was preparing to introduce a new course on the history of Israel. At the Hebrew University, however, I would be expected to revert to my former professional self as an American historian, bound to subjects that had long since ceased to excite me. In Jerusalem, of all places, I would be permanently encased in American history.

There also were compelling family concerns. My elderly father, like the biblical Jacob, yearned for his missing son. My older children, in college, had their own needs for me. Susan, away from her family, friends, and work, had been a tourist long enough. And I knew that my preference for solitude, so finely honed by my isolation in the United States, would torment me in Israel, where I most wanted to belong but never would.

I had the wisdom of my Jubilee to know that nearly fifty years as an American Jew had incapacitated me for life in the Jewish state. Without the euphoria of a religious visionary or the desperation of a new immigrant, I suffered from the fatal post-emancipation split between Western head and Jewish heart. I knew that I could never reconcile them. Instead, I secretly shared the shame of the apocryphal Zionist who, to the astonishment of his friends, never made *aliya*. Why not, they finally asked. Because, he replied wanly, if I live in Israel then I must relinquish my longing for Zion.

I could not claim, as so many American Jews did at the time, that Israel was undeserving of my refined ethical sensibilities. To the contrary: it had bestowed abundant blessings upon me. My prolonged Jewish hibernation in the diaspora ended there. I had internalized the legitimacy of the Zionist argument for the ingathering of Jewish exiles; I knew that even as an American Jew I was not exempt. I had embraced Jerusalem as though personally commanded by the Psalmist to set it "above my highest joy." I found protected Jewish space and time, where I could begin to excavate my buried Jewish self. I came to realize, as the South African novelist Dan Jacobson wrote, that Eretz Israel is "the land where each of us must try to live, for there is no other." Yet I could not, finally, leave my past behind. In the end, American freedom of choice overrode Jewish obligation.

Early in May, Susan invited my Israeli family and friends to my fiftieth birthday celebration. My cousin Zippi came with Minna, her sprightly seventy-five year-old mother, the daughter of Jacob's youngest sister. My Jerusalem cousin Barbara, one of my father's nieces, was there. Moshe and Chava broke his year of mourning to join us. Haggai and Adina, my first Israeli friends, drove down from Kfar Saba. By then I had shared so much with Haggai, a steadfast companion during all the years of my wanderings in Israel, that Shira, with the unerring insight of a three-year-old, had decided that we should be brothers. Ruth, my ulpan teacher, still patiently corrected my Hebrew grammar. Rafi regaled us with his stories. But I knew that I must abandon my fantasy of joining them in Israel.

My Jubilee year ended on Yom ha-Shoah, Holocaust remembrance day. I timed my morning walk with Shira to *gan* so that we had just crossed Azza Road, throbbing with traffic, when the memorial sirens sounded. Suddenly Jerusalem plunged into the still silence of sorrowful memory. Momentarily, my childhood was fused to hers, and to the lives of one million murdered Jewish children. I held Shira's hand too tightly, trying to squeeze this compressed legacy of Jewish history—the tragedy of annihilation coupled with the miracle of renewal—into her consciousness forever.

FROM THE HOLY CITY WE RETURNED TO OUR SUBURBAN home in the Garden City. I felt adrift. After a year in Jerusalem, the discordance of holy days in Harvard Square was unbearable. But my residual discomfort with Jewish institutional life meant that local synagogue options were even less appealing. I was trapped in the diaspora fate that I had chosen for myself.

A chance encounter led me to a nearby *minyan*, incongruously located in the annex of the local Baptist church. Its forty families were committed to traditional Jewish worship, gender egalitarianism, and each other. I was enthusiastic about the first, not uncomfortable with the second, and exceedingly wary of communal intensity. But the exuberant *davening* instantly roused me from my diaspora torpor. I stifled my residual ambivalence about community, and repressed my feelings of inadequacy in the presence of so many comfortably committed Jews.

The *minyan*, a curious mix of Jewish liturgical orthodoxy and '60s participatory democracy, slowly eroded my prolonged Jewish uneasiness in the United States. Joining as a family, newly enlarged by Rebecca's birth soon after our return from Israel, we were welcomed as a family—noteworthy only because my divorce, remarriage, and middle-aged fathering had rendered some erstwhile Cambridge congregants incapable of even the most banal civilities. Not in nearly thirty-five years, since high school and summer camp, had I belonged to anything remotely resembling a community (no less one so avowedly, and proudly, Jewish).

The structure of traditional *davening*, spiced by *minyan* enthusi-

asm, began to penetrate interior spaces that had previously opened
for me only in Israel, and rarely in synagogues there. When, occasionally, my favorite *chazzan* infused the service with traditional
Eastern European intonations and cadences, I was transported
with stunning swiftness back to my childhood, to Cantor Gorsky's
voice filtering through our living-room wall. Finally, Judaism no
longer came to me only through walls.

Yet the more comfortable that I felt in the *minyan*, the more vex-
ing were the Jewish issues that we had to confront as a family. For
example, *kashrut*. I was familiar with the principle of forbidden
foods (which included some favorite selections on every Chinese
menu); and with the prohibition against mixing meat and dairy (a
decisive rebuke to my passion for veal parmigiana). I simply had
never observed them. But *kashrut* was an implicit *minyan* expecta-
tion, even if there never were embarrassing inquiries into nuances
of observance.

For a time, we reciprocated the hospitality of our new friends by
serving fish and vegetables. By restricting ourselves to the neutral
zone between meat and dairy, we conveniently evaded the need for
separate pots and pans, dishes, and silverware. But that was only
a temporary expedient, for how often could we serve the same
meal? Susan and I began an interminable debate. She quite reasonably asked: "How can I do what I don't believe?" I quite reasonably
responded: "Why don't we just do it, and save belief for later?" The
result, predictably, was an irritable stalemate.

Then there was the looming issue of school for Shira, our older
daughter. I did not share Susan's principled commitment to public
education. But neither of us had any allegiance to Jewish day-
schools. Now we were among friends, however, for whom Jewish
education was not an after-school afterthought, as it had been
throughout our childhoods, but an integral part of their Jewish
lives. We evaded the issue, and its implications, for as long as possible.

My father was ever more puzzled by the arc of my Jewish journey. He could still rouse himself, if with diminishing frequency
and energy, for visits to Boston. But the first time that I met him at
the local train station to accompany him to the *minyan*, I winced
at his frailty. Always a vigorous, handsome man, he was now di-

minished, his gentleness submerged in melancholic sorrow. My frequent disappearances to Israel had been troubling enough for him. Now, in the United States, I actually was contemplating living a Jewish life. He never indicated whether he was pained or pleased by these reminders from his son of what, as Jacob's son, he had so long ago repudiated.

The *minyan* certainly jolted him. Nothing in his childhood Orthodoxy or adult assimilation had prepared him for this incongruous Jewish blend of traditional and egalitarian observance. It violated all his familiar boundaries of Judaism and gender. He was as startled by the sight of men, considerably younger than I, "shuckling" at prayer as he was by the sound of women reading Torah. It made no sense to him. "Is this an Orthodox *shul?*" he asked incredulously, his own comprehension of Orthodoxy completely undermined.

But my father was nothing if not ambivalent about Judaism. When he came again, with slightly diminished discomfort, he knew exactly what to do for his *aliya* and when to do it. His Hebrew intonation, with its overlapping layers of Yiddish, Pittsburgh and New York, could only have come from someone familiar with the interior of a synagogue. I was proud of him. He was better at that, I assured him, than he ever had been with a baseball glove. He smiled, tacitly conceding the point.

More than I had realized, I wanted him to share the holy days with us once, before his strength finally gave out. I yearned for a measure of Jewish reconciliation across three generations of our family history. But it was not to be. Although he could still manage smiles for his youngest granddaughters, I knew that he was drifting away. Once an inveterate walker, he could barely circumnavigate our street. I sensed that he might not return for another visit.

By his eighty-fifth birthday, a month before Rosh ha-Shanah, he no longer left his apartment. All the grandchildren gathered with us for a quiet celebration, with lox and bagels from his favorite West Side delicatessen. For some inane reason, as though it could assure his continuing presence at our table, I decided to give him an old European kiddush cup. I even bought one for him, knowing all the while that it really was for me. Then, recalling his fondness for collecting American coins from his childhood years (probably because he never had enough of them), I gave him an Indian-head penny dated 1903, the year of his birth. He hardly noticed.

For almost a year, he disappeared ever deeper inside himself. He even relaxed his tight control over family finances, which he had always guarded zealously. An astonishingly generous man, long before he ever had much to spare, he used money to express his love. I knew, all too well, how easily his generosity could become control, and how difficult it was to accept one without the other. Yet now that he was ready to relinquish everything, I was stunned. It told me that he was preparing to die. Nothing I did, in the sorrow or rage of my love, could rouse him.

A week before his eighty-sixth birthday, he was rushed to the hospital with a ruptured aneurysm. When the call came, late on a Friday afternoon, the doctor explained the urgency of surgery and the terrifying risks even if it succeeded. Amid the frenzy of telephoning family members and gathering medical information, I realized that I had been saying goodbye to my father for nearly a year. I had rehearsed his death so often that I could hardly imagine that now was the time.

When I saw him after surgery he was off the respirator and recognized me, but the prognosis was dismal. A blood clot had blocked circulation to his leg; additional surgery, including amputation, was strenuously advised. As the options narrowed and my helplessness increased, there were bruising encounters with doctors, even the most sympathetic, who were relentlessly committed to the prolongation of life at any cost. The surgeon bluntly advised me that my preoccupation with how my father would live his life, without a limb or mental acuity, was irrelevantly emotional.

During my wrenching inner debate over what treatments to authorize and what to refuse, I encountered ambiguity at every turn. When I searched for the wisdom of traditional Jewish sources, I learned that life must be preserved; quality of life considerations were extraneous. Only when a person was in the status of *goses*, in the process of dying, should life not be prolonged. By then the angels of death, sent by God, were hovering nearby and must not be obstructed. But the answer begged the question: when, precisely, would my father enter the process of dying? Was he already there? I suspected that there might be as many answers as rabbis. I had only his silence to guide me.

I also had his clock and his scale. When my father sold his business, I claimed these two artifacts as mine. I most wanted the massive old pendulum time-punch clock, framed in oak, which had registered the arrivals and departures of factory workers for nearly fifty years. Made by the International Company, the parent of IBM, it had functioned as long as my father kept it wound. It compensated for its erratic time-keeping with incessant ticks, tocks, and clicks, as though to rebuke anyone who might doubt its capabilities. For several years, the clock had ticked away on our dining-room wall, fascinating our children and their friends, who delighted in pressing the time-punch lever to hear its noisy clang.

Like my father, I dutifully wound it. I even played games with it, for it was never entirely predictable, within its weekly cycle, precisely when it would wind down. I made calculated guesses, trying not to be too eager, determined never to be tardy. It took a while for me to realize that I had come to associate the clock's tick with my father's heartbeat. Foolishly, I had arrogated to myself responsibility for keeping my father alive. From time to time, inadvertently, I was reminded that I was powerless to sustain life with a clock key. But I never lost my sense of obligation, or compulsion, to keep the clock wound. Now, when I awoke during the night, I listened for its reassuring noises.

Less important, but still worth salvaging, was the jeweler's scale, enclosed in a cumbersome wood and glass case. I collected old balance scales, charmed by their intricate design for achieving the most delicate equilibrium. This one, made by a company founded back in 1857, was not nearly as distinguished as my majestic English grocer's scale, nor at all funky like my marble-based *balance* from a Parisian flea-market. But I had kept it for sentimental reasons; a reminder, perhaps, of the career not chosen. Consigned to the basement, it competed with snow tires and storage trunks for limited space.

I struggled to decide my father's fate, tortured by the obligation that I could not evade. As a son, I still wanted my father to express his preferences, to tell me—as he always had—what to do. But we had done our elaborate pirouettes around that issue for years and I knew that he would advise me, as he finally did in a barely audible whisper, to do whatever I thought best. In New York, my daughter Pammy and I kept a sorrowful vigil, tightly bound by the painful task of parenting our fading family patriarch. Back home, I awaited any sign of cosmic guidance, but I only heard silence, punctuated by the ticking of my father's clock. The message, I intuited, was that the decision was entirely mine, which I had suspected and feared all along.

During my week of indecision about amputation, with the surgeon's deadline looming, Susan happened to move my father's scale near the door to my study. Quite early one morning, needing a respite from the incessant phone calls, I removed the scale from its unwieldy case, the better to see it from my desk. But I could not balance it. Perhaps the baseboard had warped, or my study floor sloped. I wondered if I had stumbled upon a deeper truth: that it was humanly impossible to weigh life and death issues with precision. Aided by a variety of minuscule jeweler's weights, I persevered. During odd moments, for several days, I tested the possibilities, but the needle always swung past the center, to the right, to the left, and back again.

I shifted the weights as I adjusted my calculation of the consequences of any decision about my father's fate. I added and subtracted medical opinions, my sense of my father's wishes, Jewish sources, insights from family and friends, weighing them all against my own love and fear. When I finally managed to balance the scale precisely, I felt emboldened to decide. Silent postponement, itself a decision, was too passive for me. I told the surgeon that I would not authorize further surgery. He assured me that my father would die within the month. The next day I discovered a card, buried deep inside my father's wallet, requesting that he not be kept alive by artificial means or heroic measures. I appreciated his belated guidance.

In a desperate effort to preserve some semblance of normality, I had accepted a *minyan* invitation to comment on the weekly Torah reading. My portion, by chance, was the beginning of the Book of Deuteronomy—in Hebrew, *Devarim*, from its opening lines: "These are the words," the final words that Moses would speak to the children of Israel. He knew that he would soon die; his people would enter the promised land without him. The entire book is his farewell.

Moses confronted his impending death with a sustained, impassioned exhortation. He enumerated the wondrous blessings and terrible curses that Israel would incur as it obeyed or ignored divine command. In his great lyrical song of praise to God, as in his concluding blessing to Israel, his words reach astonishing heights of poetic intensity. They are all the more remarkable from a man suffering a speech impediment, who once had doubted his ability to speak articulately to Pharoah. Perhaps Moses imagined that sheer eloquence would persuade God to relent, permitting him to enter the promised land after all.

I wondered, that *Shabbat*, what might be said when death is imminent. Which final words—commands, exhortations, warnings, wishes, fears—are spoken to those whose lives still stretch before them? How is the historical legacy to be summarized? How, at the last possible moments of life, can the meaning of a life, and the purpose of life, be conveyed? If my own Moshe (my father's Hebrew name) asked these questions, his words remained inaudible to me.

My father slipped silently away that weekend. I fought off my impulse to intervene. His nurse Daphne, who had lovingly cared for him during his final year, reassured me that I should let him go peacefully and quietly. His jeweler's scale, finally in equilibrium, remained perfectly balanced. To be absolutely certain that I had done everything I could, I wound the clock.

I had more than enough time to prepare for his death. But I was unprepared for how little difference all my preparations actually mattered. My deepest fear, given my father's age, the self-imposed isolation of his last years, and the wide dispersion of our small family, was that no one would attend his funeral. Then I would truly be alone. But favorite childhood cousins, whom I had not seen in thirty years, came. So did two of my oldest friends. The *minyan* eased my concern that there would not even be enough mourners present for me to recite *kaddish*.

My father's funeral dissolved familiar boundaries of time. My cousins now were older than their parents had been when I last saw them. As I listened to my friend Moshe chant the mournful *El Male Rachamim*, I heard vibrant echoes of Cantor Gorsky's voice. My cousin Sondra evoked hauntingly vivid memories of my father, her dearest uncle, that I never could have recaptured without her exquisite articulation. For my children, it was the first intimate family loss. For me—only child, only son—there was bittersweet comfort in a verse from Proverbs: "For the Lord reproves him whom he loves: even as a father the son in whom he delights."

As the funeral cortege turned a corner on our way to the cemetery, I caught a glimpse in my side-view mirror of a long line of headlights shining behind me, as far back as I could see. Linked in a chain of mourners, I was comforted. But I remembered that some years before, and more than once, my father had strongly expressed his preference for cremation. I may have known that it was strictly prohibited by Jewish law. Certainly I wanted to honor my father's wish. But I was troubled by the total self-effacement that it seemed to express. I could not easily evade his request, but I did not want to obey it.

Eventually, I spoke to my rabbi. Uncertain how to resolve the conflict, he referred me to Rabbi Joseph Soloveitchik, the revered *halakhic* scholar who lived in Boston. After a brief discussion with his daughter, who carefully monitored his time, the rabbi answered my call. Listening to my dilemma, he quickly responded, "That is not a problem." I felt slightly cheated. Why not, I asked. True to the rabbinical tradition of answering every question with a question, he asked: "If your parents instructed you to steal, would you become a thief?"

I had carefully chosen the cemetery, one of the oldest in Boston, for its evocation of Eastern Europe. Its slightly disheveled Old World appearance contrasted sharply with the more cultivated suburban tracts so carefully landscaped to deny death. We drove slowly past decrepit memorial chapels, behind wrought-iron fences that guarded the subdivisions allocated long ago to now defunct immigrant burial associations. Although my father devoted his entire life to eluding his past, I had decided to return him there—and, I understood, to reclaim it for myself.

In Jewish tradition, the phases of mourning and memory are

precisely demarcated: *shiva*, the first seven days; *shloshim*, the first month; *kaddish*, recited for eleven months; the gravestone unveiling during the first year; the *yahrzeit* anniversaries; and the *Yizkor* memorial service on specified holy days, especially Yom Kippur. I often wondered whether the ancient sages had been so psychologically astute as to comprehend the precise stages of grief; or whether generations of Jews had been trained to adjust their emotions to our inherited schedule.

During the week of *shiva* following the funeral, the synagogue moves, literally, to the mourner's home. The *minyan* became our extended family, feeding us and caring for our children. Friends interrupted their lives to arrive early each morning and again in the evening, for services. One of them, in mourning himself, always gave me a reassuring glance as the moment for *kaddish* neared, standing by me as we recited it together. As my home became a house of prayer, the *minyan* became my community of consolation.

On Friday, when I was feeling edgy after four days of unrelieved confinement, two friends appeared unexpectedly with a challah and flowers for *Shabbat*. They asked gently about my father, whom they had never met, and listened patiently to my torrential response. For the first time since his death, I could express my very conflicted feelings about him.

I had never doubted his love, although I always found his financial generosity to be an inadequate expression of it. So often, too, my difficult decisions had elicited his critical judgments. That still rankled, as the reference to paternal reproof in my eulogy clearly indicated. Yet, Melinda and Trudy reminded me, for the most important decision of all—his own life or death—my father had trusted me to decide wisely. He had, I knew, tried to tell me, in his own way, that with his death the boy—his boy—must finally become the man.

As *shiva* ended, grief and solace were so tightly interwoven that my loss had become the source of a deeper identification than I had ever known. A friend stayed late that final morning to walk with me around the block for my symbolic re-entry into the world that I had abruptly left one week earlier. I felt disoriented. I had never been without my father. Nor had I ever belonged to a Jewish community. Now my father was dead, but his death had enclosed me within a living community of Jews. He might not have approved, but I still wished that I could have tried to persuade him that it all made sense.

After my father's death, I needed to find some way to preserve the continuity that I knew was irretrievably lost. Once again, I became preoccupied with *kashrut*. Susan and I had already taken halting steps: we banished forbidden foods; we restricted ourselves to kosher meat; when the nearby kosher bakery caused a local scandal by selling *traif* products, we joined the customer exodus to buy our challah elsewhere. But *kashrut*, ultimately, must be either/or, not both. It cannot be resolved in classic American fashion: do whatever pleases you. How could we belong to a community if we distanced ourselves from it?

Why, we debated interminably, must we obey rules that were anything but self-evident? Why is chicken "meat"? What about swordfish, which loses its early scales (a requirement for edible fish)? Could our wooden-handled silverware be made kosher? And our rubber-coated dishwasher racks? Could we explain to our children the distinction between Hydrox cookies (kosher) and Oreos (*traif*)? And what did all this have to do with holiness, the biblical justification for *kashrut*? Or my father?

We remained partners, my father and I, in a continuing generational dialogue, never quite made explicit between us. For him, *kashrut* was something to leave behind, an uncomfortable reminder of the immigrant Orthodoxy of his family. Precisely according to the promise of emancipation embodied in the American dream, he had shed the ghetto rags of Pittsburgh's Hill district, first for the middle-class respectability of Forest Hills and then for Upper East Side affluence.

For my father, Judaism was an obstacle to be overcome, not an identification to be cherished. He had a fierce attachment to American national symbols and the sentimental patriotism that accompanied them that was so characteristic of immigrant children. Even the awkward musical cadences of the Star Spangled Banner brought tears to his eyes. He loved marching bands and Sousa tunes and dragged me to countless parades when I was a child. Too young for World War I and too old for World War II, he compensated with patriotic fervor for what his good fortune had spared him.

As long as I avoided the stigma of intermarriage, still vestigially strong even in our family, he seemed satisfied. I was encouraged to be as minimal a Jew as I cared to be. Indeed, the more minimal the better. Lox and bagels, Jewish wry, and reverence for F.D.R. sufficed. Like most other American Jews who internalized emancipation norms, I had persuaded myself that my identity an an American and a Jew was a seamless unity. The essence of Judaism, I had learned, was its inherent compatibility with enlightened American liberalism. It had never occurred to me to wonder why the Jewish texture of my life was so threadbare.

Had I ever been so thoughtless as to inquire what my father had relinquished along the way, he would have been uncomprehending. I could hardly have asked, for long before I understood his Jewish compromises I had internalized them as my own. And yet: if Jewish ambivalence was my father's legacy to me, Jewish denial was not. He even managed to bestow some genuine Jewish blessings along the way, infrequent and attenuated though they might be: our journey together to the Lower East Side for my bar mitzvah *tallit*; his trip to Israel to affirm his bond with the remnants of Jacob's Romanian family. Certainly he did not embellish Jacob's voice. And we collaborated for many years to silence it by enclosing it within American walls that left it all but inaudible. Until, in Israel, it finally reverberated inside me so powerfully that I could not elude it. I heard it again in the *minyan*, when it enfolded me after my father's death.

"Memory of the past," historian Yosef Hayim Yerushalmi has noted, always was "a central component of the Jewish experience." The Torah repeatedly admonishes the children of Israel, "*zachor*" (remember); alternatively, but no less insistently, "*lo tishkach*" (do not forget). The symbols, gestures, and words of Jewish religious ritual, within the structure of the Jewish calendar, constantly rekindle memory. In the modern era, however, Jewish memory has severely atrophied. The remembering Jew has been replaced by the Jew for whom Jewishness has become an endless array of personal choices.

Except for the aging relatives of my childhood, with their Yiddish expressions and Old World fondness for strong tea, I always lived comfortably among Jews whose memory loss matched mine. Slightly embarrassed by our elders but unable to understand why, we had no wish to remember what our American upbringing taught us to forget. Like so many second-generation fathers, mine diligently pursued his assigned task: to obliterate Eastern European Jewish memory. I was the crown jewel of his success, an enlightened American Jew who suffered from a debilitating case of Jewish amnesia. I knew that a good Jew was a Jew who transcended Judaism.

It all made sense, until Israel suddenly jarred loose all the compromises and evasions that I had so carefully layered to insulate my Jewish self. Israel, at first, was Jewish memory, releasing all the suppressed Jewish images of my childhood. As if in Ezekiel's vision of the dry bones miraculously restored to life, the skeletons of my departed relatives appeared as living Jews on the streets of Jerusalem. I saw my stocky old aunts in their laced black shoes and my balding uncles with their flashing gold teeth, my grandmother with her long hair braided into a tight bun, and my bearded grandfather who had never spoken to me. I explored their neighborhoods, visited their *shtieblach*, shopped in their markets, and ate in restaurants that still served the indigestible dinners that they once had cooked for me. In Israel I finally understood why, although Jacob was the immigrant, I had always shared his feeling of living as an alien in someone else's country.

At first, I was too busy with my own memories to confront the larger meaning of Israel as the reconstituted national memory of the Jewish people. A country younger than I am (to the astonishment of my children), its ancient history makes the beginnings of Western civilization, to say nothing of American history, seem almost contemporary by comparison. The point came home to me one day in Harvard Yard, where tourists often gather in their pilgrimage from the Old North Church to Lexington Green to venerate the American colonial past. I overheard a visitor marvel at a building nearly two hundred years old. I had just returned from Jerusalem, where the Burnt House, an evocative two-thousand-year-old remnant of the Roman war, had recently been excavated and restored. I knew that I identified more closely with the Zealots who fought against Titus than with the Patriots who battled the Redcoats. Israel had begun to mend the Jewish historical synapses that had atrophied in our family during three generations in the United States.

But which Israel? Not the land of milk and honey, the light unto the nations. That Israel was populated by *halutzim* who looked like Paul Newman in *Exodus*, wearing *kova tembels* by day, dancing the *hora* all night, and piloting their tanks and planes to astonishing victories the next morning. I never was captivated by those mythological images of the Jewish state. In the Israel I encountered after the Six Day War, I glimpsed flickering remnants of Jewish memory on the edge of modern oblivion. My Israel was not a projection of American liberal fantasies, but an escape from the Jewish self-denial that so often accompanied them.

My deepening attachment to Israel had nothing to do with Labor Zionism, the ruling ideology of statehood for thirty years. I was engaged, instead, by the contentious struggle over whether Israel would define itself as a state of the Jews or as a Jewish state. This posed a dilemma for many American Jews, whose Zionism depended upon Israel emulating secular liberal fashion in the West. The more Jewish that Israel became, and the sharper the conflict between Jewish and liberal values, the more discomfort for Jews in the American diaspora.

As I began to navigate my way through two countries, two cultures, two calendars, two languages, and two histories, the boundary between what was American and what was Jewish sharpened. In the United States I felt like a stranger in a foreign place; Israel had become my country of refuge. Yet even Israel could not avoid the wrenching encounter between Jewish history and Western modernity. Indeed, its most acute political and cultural conflicts find their source in precisely this tension. The claim of secular Israelis, that living in Israel and speaking Hebrew is all that is demanded of Jews, never persuaded me. These Israelis, lacking religious sensibility, dismissive of Jewish diaspora history between 70 c.e. and 1948, and addicted to Western cultural fashion, are as Jewishly impoverished as the *galut* Jews they delight in demeaning. I was intrigued by the other Israel. In this Israel, remote from the fashionable cafés of Tel Aviv, the university heights of Mt. Scopus, the orange groves of the coastal plain, and the beaches of Eilat, I encountered Jewish memory. Here, in the Old City, in the shtetl neighborhoods of Jerusalem, in Judean hilltop settlements, in Kiryat Arba and Hebron, liberalism and Judaism seemed like an odd couple, the accidental union of a shotgun marriage in the modern era. Away from ersatz Israeli outposts of Western culture and Jewish normalization, I began to confront assumptions about religion, politics; liberalism, and loyalty that had always defined my American Jewish identity.

Like most American Jews, I had worshipped fervently at Thomas Jefferson's "wall of separation" between church and state. Its secular sleight-of-hand converted Christmas into a "national" holiday and Sunday into a neutral "day of rest." Religion was consigned to the nether realms of irrelevance, but the Christian framework of American culture remained firmly in place. Singing Christmas carols in public school was a lesson in hypocrisy that any American Jew of my generation could easily absorb, as we tucked Judaism into the private recesses of our indifference. The principle of religion-state separation made perfect sense to me for precisely as long as Judaism was marginal to my own life.

I never suspected that the separationist principle itself was deeply embedded in Christianity. (Jesus, not Moses, had distinguished between what must be rendered to God and to Caesar.) Or that its adoption in the United States might have had more to do with Protestant piety and politics than with religious tolerance. It was enough, as Jews, that we were Americans. If that required a pledge of allegiance to a principle that contradicted our own history and identity as Jews, we would gladly offer it.

The separationist position, I realized in Israel, expresses a curiously American form of Jewish self-denial. Its primary function, quite contrary to Jewish teaching, is to separate religion from life, thereby privatizing and trivializing it. I finally understood that there is nothing neutral about any of this. In Israel, it is as natural for observant Jews to be on the street as it is for Jews to be observant at home. Rabbis are in the Knesset as members, not chaplains. Religious symbols—*mezzuzahs, menorahs,* and *sukkas*—adorn public buildings. Government support for religious education is not seriously questioned. In a Jewish state, the separation of religion and state makes no sense at all. Separation, after all, is a secular adaptation of Christian theology, not a Jewish precept.

Israeli Orthodoxy, of course, is anathema to most American Jews. Rabbis (as Theodor Herzl pointedly suggested in *The Jewish State*) belong in their temples, not in politics. American Jews were enraged, just a decade ago, when Israeli rabbis insisted that any convert to Judaism who claims the right to immigrate to Israel under its Law of Return must follow the conversion procedure of Jewish religious law—as interpreted by Orthodox rabbis. Who, Israeli rabbis were asking, is a Jew? We, they insisted, will decide.

The number of American Jews, let alone converts, who actually make *aliya* is infinitesimal. But that hardly matters. The provocation for this Jewish family feud is intermarriage. Endemic in the United States (where more than half the Jews who marry now intermarry), it accelerates the transformation of Judaism into a casual, ephemeral American preference. Among the intermarried, there are relatively few conversions, and even fewer that could be considered valid according to Jewish law. If the Orthodox rabbinate in Israel had its way, the Jewish credentials of these converts would be implicitly suspect. A sterner rebuke to American "pro-choice Judaism" could hardly be imagined.

Orthodox rabbinical resistance to intermarriage makes perfect sense to me. I may retain a measure of surprise, dating from the years when I had been taught that Judaism was a disability, that anyone who is not a Jew might wish to become one. But those who do, it seems reasonable to expect, should respect the admission standards of the club they wish to join. Why should American Jews expect a Jewish state to validate their distinctively American (inter)marriage patterns? Orthodox rabbis, the guardians of Jewish religious memory, make much the stronger Jewish argument.

I continued to live in the United States, but its language and culture were increasingly foreign to me. I began to read newspapers and magazines inside out, turning first to Middle Eastern news. Subscribing to more Israeli than American periodicals, I developed a better sense of politics there than here. My children quickly learned that my sternest "Shhh!" meant that I was hearing news from, or about, Israel. One morning in *minyan*, a friend who happened to glance at my watch wondered why the alarm was set for 5:23. That was not alarm time, I responded, but Israel time. His evident surprise momentarily puzzled me, for it suddenly made explicit the parallel time zones that partitioned my own interior life.

As political disagreements increasingly pulled American and Israeli Jewry apart during the 1980s, I often felt unAmerican. I was neither Israeli nor Orthodox, but I had shed the mask of liberal universalism worn by American Jews to blend into the American mainstream. Liberalism, I knew all too well, easily served as an exit from Judaism. To locate the entrance, after so many years outside, I needed a different Jewish perspective. Once I found it, in Israel, my commitment to liberal tenets eroded—as did my sense of American national loyalty.

The arrest of Jonathan Pollard as an Israeli spy crystallized my uneasiness. It was easy, and certainly justified, to chastize Israel. Its folly in choosing Pollard (or any American Jew) for its dirty work of espionage was evident. Yet the glaring harshness of Pollard's life sentence, a punishment far more severe than any recently meted out to career spies who happened not to be Jewish, barely stirred American Jewry. Nor did American Jews seem perturbed once it became public knowledge that Secretary of Defense Caspar Weinberger (whose father was born a Jew) had applied unseemly pressure on the presiding judge for the maximum sentence, the better to punish the Jewish state for its perfidy.

The American Jewish community, renowned for its reflexive protests against injustice (to others), responded to a glaring injustice to one of its own with abject silence. I knew the sound of that silence. I heard it as a boy during the feverish peak of anti-Communist frenzy, when Julius and Ethel Rosenberg were convicted and executed for conspiring to commit atomic espionage for the Soviet Union. I never knew whether the Rosenbergs were guilty, but I always remembered the frightened silence that descended over our family as their fate was being decided.

In the Rosenberg trial, the prosecutors and presiding judge were Jews. Their complicity with the government, to protect the innocence of American Jewry and their own, had eluded me at the time. Now, many years later, an appellate court upheld Pollard's sentence. Both judges in the majority (including the future Supreme Court appointee, Ruth Bader Ginsburg) were Jews. I understood.

It took an Israeli political scientist, Shlomo Avineri, to pry open the loyalty issue for closer scrutiny. Avineri sharply rebuked American Jews for their "nervousness, insecurity and . . . cringing." Why had spokesmen for American Jewish organizations rushed to distance themselves from Pollard? Because, Avineri suggested, they still were tormented by the endemic anxieties of Jewish life in *galut*: "ambivalence, alienation, homelessness."

American Jewish leaders, silent witnesses to Pollard's fate, responded with predictable outrage to Avineri's identification of American Jewry with other frightened diaspora communities in Jewish history. Yet Pollard, so embarrassing for Jews, was virtually ignored by other Americans. While American Jews anticipated an anti-Semitic backlash, few non-Jews even were aware that Pollard had spied for Israel. (Many believed that he was a Soviet spy.) Jews were far likelier than non-Jews to conclude that his sentence was excessively harsh, but their silent acquiescence exposed a reluctance to criticize the American government on a Jewish issue.

Jonathan Pollard's espionage confronted me with my own estrangement from the United States. I did not feel threatened, as a Jew, by Pollard. Indeed, his actions shamed me less than the conduct of my own government and the alacrity with which the Jewish community turned its back on him. Nor was the Pollard case unique: several years later, during the Crown Heights pogrom against Hasidic Jews, the same American Jewish leadership was frightened, yet again, into the same shameful silence. Hasidic victims were too Jewish for American Jewish liberals to defend against Black violence.

Like most diaspora Jews, I had internalized Jeremiah's advice to the Jews in Babylonian exile: "seek the peace of the city into which I have caused you to be carried away captives . . . for in its peace shall you have peace." Yet somewhere I had crossed a boundary into emotional exile. I often felt like a double agent, for my deepest affections lay elsewhere. How much moral distance, I wondered, separated exile from espionage? What did loyalty—to the United States, to Judaism, to Israel—require of an American Jew?

Troubled by my American disaffection, I had some distressing flashes of recollection to my graduate-school enounter with that crusty Boston aristocrat, Henry Adams. At the end of the nineteenth century, Adams plunged into despair about American society. His Brahmin world had been undermined by commerce, finance, and immigrants—by people like my grandparents. As befitted his class, Adams defended the American traditions that his family had played so vital a role in defining by blaming everything on "infernal Jewry." He could not escape the "Jew atmosphere" that surrounded him in the United States, he confessed in his *Education*. He felt displaced by the "furtive Yacoob or Ysaac still reeking of the Ghetto." The Jew, Adams wrote to a friend, "makes me creep."

Although there were no Puritans or Patriots in my lineage, I had always assumed that two generations of American forebears sufficed. Certainly no one I knew, until I met a German Jew in college, had more. Adams's fears about our ancestors notwithstanding, successive generations of American Jews had internalized their Jewish handicap, played by American rules, and struggled to surmount the obstacles of prejudice and discrimination. They remained convinced, often against abundant evidence to the contrary, that success was the assured prize for hard work. American society rewarded merit; failure was a personal, not a social, defect. Believing success to be within their reach, they achieved it.

Their achievement, I knew, had shaped my own meritocratic vision. The three-generation progression of my Jewish contemporaries seemed inevitable. Our grandfathers, Eastern European immigrants all, were unskilled workers; our fathers, born in the United States, succeeded in business; we were destined, as their sons, to become professionals. And we did.

After twenty-five years of professorial life, however, my meritocratic fantasy had become as obsolete as Adams's Brahmin nostalgia. As a Jew, I discovered upon my return to Wellesley from my
sabbatical year in Israel that I had suddenly become politically in-
correct. Consigned to the white male patriarchy, the newly de-
spised American ruling class, I encountered an astonishing expec-
tation: I should sacrifice meritocratic principle, academic freedom,
and even historical veracity to placate the demands of aggrieved
minorities and compliant administrators.

I was often asked by friends whose careers in law, medicine,
management consulting, and other safe occupations spared them
the wounds of academic trench warfare, whether there was any
truth to all the bizarre stories they were reading about the relentless campus pressures for politically correct thought. They fondly
recalled intellectual freedom as not only the academic ideal but,
more than occasionally, even its reality. By the 1990s, however, that
time had become a historical relic, with about as much inspirational power as phrenology or pre-Galilean astronomy. Galileo, I
hastened to add, was merely a dead white European male. Like
Socrates, Shakespeare, Dickens, and others of their ilk, he was in-
herently suspect to those whose only categories of significance
were race and gender.

I could regale friends endlessly with glimpses of life in the academic wonderland. Not all that long after 1984 (as Orwell would
have appreciated), academic departments at Wellesley, as elsewhere, were instructed by administrators to recruit candidates
from preferred minorities. (Jews, less than three percent of the
American population, did not qualify.) Our own search commit-
tees were advised to bring minority candidates to the campus for
job interviews, even if they must be put ahead of more qualified
whites. After some inept candidates were humiliated, the college
decided to fund special positions for members of designated minorities to spare them competition with other applicants. (No Jews
need apply.)

All this and multiculturalism too, I informed my glazed listen-
ers, had become part of the natural academic order. The plague of
multiculturalism, the gradual recasting of entire academic disci-
plines to satisfy victimized minorities, eventually penetrated my

own classroom. In a course on freedom of expression (one of the lingering vestiges of my liberal past), during a discussion of the Nazis in Skokie, I happened in passing to identify the Holocaust as an episode unique in history for the targeting of an entire people, based upon their "race," for extermination.

An African-American student suddenly erupted in anger. She demanded equal recognition for the "six million" African slaves who had died onboard ship during their wretched Middle Passage to the United States. I was startled by her claim. I explained to her that it was the Nazi Holocaust that had created "six million" as a number of uniquely horrific significance; and that no reasonably accurate historical estimate of slave deaths in transit, during all the centuries of American servitude, even remotely approached that number. As awful as slavery surely was, enslavement—which constrained traders and owners to protect their investment in chattel property—must be distinguished from Nazi genocide.

Several days later, I received a note from the college dean advising me that a student had complained about how I had treated her in class. I was, she alleged, "hindering diversity." A meeting, in the presence of the affirmative action officer, was requested. So began a bizarre and wearying process, lasting for months. My creative energies were depleted writing memos to academic administrators, compelled by bureaucratic imperatives of their own design to treat any allegation of political incorrectness as a high crime. They seemed blissfully unaware that academic freedom might actually protect an instructor who spoke truth in his own classroom.

Even in a multicultural world, I tried to explain, historical veracity should not casually be abandoned to appease the aggrieved. Were faculty now expected to sacrifice scholarly integrity, I wondered, just as we had already been asked to dispense with meritocratic hiring, also for "worthier" goals? But I could not persuade the dean until, in a postscript of frustration, I finally uttered the magic word: "lawyer." Then, with remarkable alacrity, she instructed my student in the virtues of academic freedom and dismissed her complaint.

My experience, trivial though it was, exemplified the politically correct and historically perverse hijacking of the Holocaust by enemies of the Jews. The PLO had already begun to appropriate Jewish symbols for its propaganda war against Israel. For a new generation who knew not Hitler, that made it easier to equate Jews with Nazis and Palestinian refugee camps with Auschwitz. Now it became the conventional wisdom, in some campus precincts, to believe that what Nazis did to Jews (if, indeed, they did anything at all) was all but indistinguishable from American racism. The Holocaust, too insignificant for anyone to notice at the time, attracted remarkable interest once Jews could be displaced as its victims.

In a multicultural environment, victimization was the ultimate source of empowerment—and the newest breeding ground of anti-Semitism. According to the prevailing terms of political correctness, Jews were consigned to the category of white privileged majority. There they were placed in the dock of vengeful judgment for every historical sin—from the enslavement of Africans to the annihilation of Palestinians—that the febrile imagination of academic charlatans could conjure.

One of my own Wellesley colleagues, a faithful disciple of Louis Farrakhan and the Nation of Islam, became a national media celebrity for nothing more than anti-Semitic ramblings in academic disguise. College administrators from Wellesley to Howard fatuously defended the academic freedom to slander Jews, while declining even to identify anti-Semitism as a problem. The Jewish vanishing act on American campuses was orchestrated by precisely those good-hearted liberals (Jews so conspicuous among them) who proclaimed their commitment to multicultural diversity. For Jews, surely, this was one of the more perverse ironies of our politically correct times.

The Persian Gulf war of 1991 provided a brief respite of American Jewish solidarity with Israel after years of deepening disenchantment with the politics and culture of the Jewish state. From the moment that the first Iraqi SCUD missiles thudded into Tel Aviv, the anxiety of American Jews for the safety of Israel was palpable. Everyone I knew worried about the fate of their Israeli families and friends who had become the targets of Saddam Hussein's reign of terror. But other feelings, far more tangled, slowly surfaced.

I felt discomforted, as a Jew, that while Israelis were in danger I was safe in the United States. I thought that I had resolved this conflict when I left Israel after my Jubilee sabbatical. I was wrong.

"We Are One!" That compelling cliché, for so long the motto of American Jews, had never sounded more hollow. As deep a longing as it might express for a close identification with Israel, it had always camouflaged the wide chasm between the diaspora and the Jewish state. The Gulf War, like previous Middle Eastern crises, momentarily roused American Jews to Jewish unity. But it only heightened my uneasiness. Where was my proper place as a Jew?

On the *Shabbat* following the first SCUD attacks, our *minyan* was filled (as were many synagogues) with Jews who came to find solace with each other and express their solidarity with Israel. It was very comforting. The *chazzan* made a spontaneous decision to recite *Tefila le-shalom Medinat Israel*, the prayer for the peace of the State of Israel. Its opening words cast a solemn spell: "Our Father who is in heaven, Protector and Redeemer of Israel, bless the State of Israel."

I was quickly jolted, however, by its sustained plea for "the whole house of Israel, in all the lands of their dispersion." That meant us. For us, in particular, God was entreated: "Speedily let them walk upright to Zion your city, to Jerusalem your dwelling place, as it is written in the Torah of your servant Moses: 'Even if you are dispersed in the uttermost parts of the world, from there the Lord your God will gather and fetch you . . . [and] bring you into the land which your fathers possessed and you shall possess it.' " I wondered whether it was God's responsibility to get us there, or ours.

I might have let the issue subside but for yet another disturbing essay by Professor Avineri, the self-appointed Israeli conscience of American Jewry. The Gulf crisis, he wrote, raised yet again the issue of "solidarity" between American Jews and Israel. "When missiles fall on Israel," Avineri observed, "Jews all over the world agonize with us. But how many have decided to be with us at this moment?" Did "solidarity" only mean financial and emotional support, "or does it have an existential dimension?" Diaspora Jews and their leaders, he knew, "chose not to be with us at a moment of clear and imminent danger."

Avineri could hardly have stated the issue more bluntly or more painfully for American Jews—or, at least, for me. From Zionist premises, I knew his critique was if anything too narrow, not too sweeping. For if Jews belong in Israel, then a moment of unusual danger is no exception. As Jews we are obligated, even during ordinary times, to be there. Yet I also knew—from two years of attempting to navigate Israeli ministries, obtain telephone service from Bezeq, drive safely from Jerusalem to Tel Aviv, and pour milk from plastic bags—how much that was really asking.

By then, all the arguments were familiar: from the withering away of the diaspora to the centrality of Zion; from the abundant evidence of Jewish tenacity and creativity outside the Land of Israel to the significance of the Jewish national revival in the historic homeland; from the opportunities afforded American Jews in their land of freedom to the illusions of Jewish security in foreign lands ("slavery in freedom," according to Ahad Ha'Am), cherished by every flourishing Jewish community from ancient Babylon to modern Berlin.

The usual rejoinders of American Jews—variations on the theme that we can best serve Israel by remaining in the United States, the better to lobby the American government and contribute money to the Jewish state—sounded exceedingly hollow. It was far too convenient a division of labor: Israelis must bear the burden of preserving Jewish national life, enduring the risks and hardships that accompany it, while American Jews write checks, telephone the White House, and publish letters to the editor—if that.

But Israel, according to the prescient warning of the literary scholar Harold Fisch just a year before the Gulf war, "is a problem that will not go away." Why not? Because "it is inside us and not simply 'over there.' " It certainly was inside me. Not Israel alone, but all the unresolved issues of modernity for Jews, for which Israel was the living Jewish metaphor. Zionism, at perhaps the last possible historical moment, had offered a secular Jewish alternative to external oppression and internal disintegration. Herzl had warned Jews to leave the diaspora, because "your existence as Jews will come to an end there." But American Jews did not, could not, never would believe that Herzl's warning applied to them. Yet Israel, as Fisch wrote, "carries the burden of Jewish history on its back." So Hillel Halkin's impassioned inquiry, in his *Letters to an American Jewish Friend*, tormented me during the Gulf war: "Why don't you really come home?"

A genial rabbi, brushing my torment away, suggested that "Zion" might not even be there, in Israel. Surely there were many more sparks of holiness in our *minyan* than in Eilat, or perhaps all of Tel Aviv. He was probably right. And Israel, other liberal Jewish friends admonished me, was governed by militant settlers and religious fanatics; therefore it was hardly worthy of our support, to say nothing of our presence. And so on. But the truth of it, I suspected, was that we American Jews, the creatures of our assorted comforts, are unwilling to risk our life, liberty, or pursuit of happiness in Israel, even for SCUD-free beaches and cafés in Tel Aviv.

That might be a plausible American answer, but it hardly was a satisfactory Jewish response. Indeed, if there was a persuasive rejoinder to Avineri's question, I could not discover it. American claims of Jewish solidarity sounded hollow indeed. Israel remained a continuing problem for American Jews, "inside us." That, I knew, was the price that we were obligated, as diaspora Jews, to pay.

Like other American Jews who felt the pain of their distance from Israel during the Gulf war, I returned as soon as I conveniently could. A few months later, waiting at Ben-Gurion airport for my Jerusalem *sherut*, I watched a group of newly arrived Soviet Jews, exhausted, confused, huddled together for security, barricaded behind their trunks and suitcases. Even children were subdued by the wrenching shock of their displacement. Several older men, conspicuously well dressed, displayed their World War II battle ribbons on their jacket lapels as though needing to say: once I was someone. I overheard an El Al worker murmur to his partner: "*Y'tziat Mitzrayim.*" Precisely: I was witnessing another exodus, another journey to the promised land, a modern reenactment of the formative saga of Jewish history.

Within a week, all Israel experienced the enduring reality of biblical metaphors. The astonishing rescue of Ethiopian Jewry during Operation Solomon prompted Israelis to describe, incessantly and with wonder, how once again in a moment of supreme danger the "waters" (this time in Ethiopia) had miraculously parted to permit the safe passage of Jews on their journey from exile to Israel. Few Israelis seemed unaffected by the literal reenactment of this primal episode in Jewish memory.

Before the euphoria had subsided, Secretary of State James Baker sharply criticized Jewish settlements in Judea and Samaria as the greatest "obstacle to peace" in the Middle East. What passed for American diplomatic wisdom was perceived in Israel as a rather ludicrous distortion of regional realities. With telling irony, a cartoonist depicted a procession of such "peaceful" Arab statesmen as King Fahd of Saudi Arabia, carrying an olive branch; and President Assad of Syria, holding a dove. (Perhaps charitably, he omitted Saddam Hussein, curled up with a lamb; or a Hamas sheik beneath a halo). The Secretary of State, leading the march, had suddenly halted his Peace Now parade at "the obstacle," a line of settlement dwellings quite as menacing as a row of Monopoly houses.

As an American historian, I knew about American diplomatic efforts, dating back to the Truman and Eisenhower administrations, to undermine Jewish immigration and settlement in Israel lest the presence of Jews offend Arab sensibilities. As an American Jew, I felt shame and anger with my own government. I decided to see for myself.

Whenever I returned to Judea and Samaria, I felt the resonant power of the historic and geographic homeland of the Jewish people. Traveling through the Judean hills between Jerusalem and Hebron is a journey through Jewish history, which began in the Land of Israel where the Jewish settlers now live. For a millennium, Jewish civilization flourished precisely here. I could only wonder with dismay at how little it all mattered to so many Jews, not only outside but even inside Israel.

The claims and counterclaims flew back and forth endlessly: Arab demography, Jewish democracy, national security, land for peace. Yet none of the arguments against these newest Jewish settlements was new. They had all been used to oppose earlier Jewish settlements, whether in Rishon LeZion, Zichron Yakov, or Degania—everywhere that Jews had come to live. For all too many Arabs, there was no distinction between new Jewish settlements and old kibbutzim—or, as Saddam Hussein's SCUDs had vividly demonstrated, Tel Aviv. I wondered why any Jew would consider the Jewish settlements of Efrat, Kedumim, or Kiryat Arba less legitimate than neighboring Arab villages. It seemed at least as plausible to label Beit Umman and Beit Fajjar as Palestinian obstacles to peace in Judea.

With Dov, a genial and thoughtful Orthodox settler, I returned to Judea for the first time since the beginning of the *intifada*. On a warm May morning, normal life prevailed. Arab schoolgirls walked to school, shopkeepers chatted outside with early customers. Shepherds, oblivious to morning traffic, guided their flocks of sheep and goats along the roadside. Israelis commuted to work in nearby Jerusalem. Military vehicles patrolled the road. I had traveled this way too many times not to feel its familiarity; yet I could hardly pretend that this was an ordinary place. Dov's car had plastic windows and a shatterproof windshield; he maintained frequent radio contact with his office; and he kept a gun in his glove compartment. That was fine. Similarly protected, I might feel almost as comfortable driving through Harlem or south central Los Angeles.

We stopped first at Bat Ayin, settled by eight families just a year earlier. Joined now by thirty others, they live in caravans on a hilltop with a spectacular view that spans the Mediterranean coast from Gaza to Tel Aviv. The settlement is something of an oddity, for its members are not only committed Zionists but passionate Hasidim. Tzvi, a tall, trim man with intense blue eyes, welcomed us to his new home. His photograph album vividly documented the brief history of Bat Ayin, from the arrival of the first caravan (his own) on the empty hill that would become the settlement.

His pictures sparked a flash of recognition to the old watchtower-and-stockade encampments that by now are flourishing *kibbutzim*. When Tzvi told me that he had grown up on a kibbutz, it struck me that despite his ideological distance from kibbutz life, he was in his own way replicating the pioneering efforts of his parents and theirs. Here was new Zionist wine in old Jewish bottles. Just how old I learned when Dov and I explored the remnants of an ancient wine-press and Second Temple *mikvah*, discovered when the road to Bat Ayin was bulldozed. This empty hilltop was even more appropriate for Jewish habitation than its newest settlers had imagined, for Jews had already lived here more than two millennia ago.

The Jews of Hebron are routinely denounced as the most mis-guided of religious fanatics. But here, where Jews had returned af-ter the Six Day War to rebuild the venerable community destroyed by Arab terror in 1929, I could hardly imagine a more appropriate place for Jews to live. At a cluster of caravans on the Tel Rumeida ridge within the city, Chaim invited us inside to talk and eat. He brushed aside my apology for our unexpected intrusion with the genial reminder that it was in the spirit of Abraham, greeting the angels, to extend hospitality to strangers.

Chaim, like most other Hebron Jews I met that day, contradicted conventional liberal stereotypes. An Orthodox Jew, he was neither wild-eyed nor uzi-toting, but a quite normal young man who, with his family, lived a normal Jewish life in a rather abnormal place. "Why do you live in Hebron," I asked him. "Because Jewish history began here," Chaim instantly responded. He added, quietly: "The tree with the deepest roots is the strongest tree."

Hebron can be intensely uncomfortable for Jewish visitors. Arab hostility is undisguised, and I knew that our car (with Israeli plates) presented an inviting target. Outside the five-hundred-year-old Avraham Avinu synagogue, standing with my back to the Arab casbah, I felt unpleasant twinges of fear, despite the conspicuous presence of Israeli soldiers on an adjacent rooftop. There we were, Jews wearing *kippot*, standing at a synagogue in the center of the most fiercely Islamic city west of the Jordan river. At that moment, yearning to be safely inside, I could understand why Jews might prefer Haifa. But why should Arab hostility be sufficient to exclude Jews who wish to live here?

Chaim knew why he lived in Hebron; but why, I wondered, was I there? Why did I persist in returning, as if on an obligatory pil-grimage, to such a menacing place? I was hardly accustomed to courting danger. Yet I had repeatedly visited Hebron, with assorted Israeli and Arab companions, as though I needed to come here to unravel some nagging interior mystery that I had yet to identify.

There had been other times when I felt a similar, irresistible pull to a hostile, even terrifying, place. In Alabama, outside the Dexter Avenue Baptist Church, talking with Rev. Martin Luther King, Jr. while whites shouted angry insults. In Germany, while riding the train from Munich to Dachau and spending the night in a tawdry inn near the camp. Perhaps I had needed Montgomery to confront the legacy of American racism and Dachau to face down my childhood terrors of the Holocaust.

But why Hebron? I went there, surely, to discover what had been expunged, at an early age, when I learned to suppress the claims of Jewish memory. Here, if anywhere in the Land of Israel, that memory can be reactivated. Hebron, after all, was the very first patriarchal foothold in the land of Israel. Here King David ruled before he made Jerusalem the capitol of a united Israel. In Hebron, I could experience the continuing struggle of Jews, with an intensity undiminished since Isaac and Ishmael divided Abraham's patrimonial legacy, to fulfill their ancient destiny in their own homeland. I knew how close I had come to abdicating my own claim to a share of Jewish history. In Hebron I could measure my meandering journey from American assimilation to Jewish identification.

My empathy with the newer settlers of Hebron, rather than the older settlers of Tel Aviv, left my liberal Jewish friends aghast. They were certain that I had betrayed my critical faculties for a band of religious fanatics. Surely I must realize, as a historian, that Israelis (like seventeenth-century Puritans and nineteenth-century pioneers) had stolen land from its indigenous inhabitants; they had (like Mississippi racists) deprived Arabs of civil rights; and (like American soldiers in Viet Nam) they had brutalized innocent victims of their own illicit occupation. When I rejected these false analogies, insisting that the Middle East was not the Middle West and that Israel could hardly "occupy" its own historic homeland, I was invariably dismissed as a hopelessly misguided zealot.

We engaged in endless debate, shouting across the chasm of our Jewish disagreement. To my protagonists, any Judaism that contradicted liberal tenets was incomprehensible. Indeed, Jewish history removed from an American frame of reference made no sense at all to them. I understood their liberal perspective; it had once been mine. But I had crossed a Jewish boundary beyond the limits of liberal tolerance. For my transgression, I became an intellectual pariah.

Nonetheless, I admired the fierce struggle of the settlers, standing on what Amos Oz aptly called "the brink of lunatic daring," to reconstruct a Jewish synthesis that modernity had all but destroyed. These Jews, who repudiated the consequences of two centuries of Western assimilation, challenged the ideological link between liberalism and Judaism, the primary source of Jewish disintegration in the modern era. Their covenantal consciousness still bound them to the timeless relationship in Judaism between God, land, and people.

I had left my father's house too late, and too encumbered by modernity, ever to join them. But I had learned too much Jewish history not to respect the undiminished passion of their Jewish commitment. Among these Jews whose Judaism was least like mine, I always felt replenished. Secular Jews like Oz might despise their "nationalistic-religious fantasy." Indeed, he dismissed the biblical allure that impelled Jews to return to Judea and Samaria as a cursed dream, shared by all "madmen burning with prophetic light." Yet who were the Zionist pioneers of the fabled second *aliya* if not such "madmen"? I had lived for a long time in Oz's own fantasy land of "spiritual pluralism," in "an open, creative society" aspiring to be "progressive and just." It was quite wonderful for Jews, but the destructive consequences for Judaism were appalling.

With relatively few (mostly Orthodox) exceptions among Israelis I met over the years, only Jewish settlers retained the passion—call it zeal—that once must have inspired the early Zionists. Those pioneers from Russia and Poland, committed to a vision of Jewish national redemption completely without historical precedent, had struggled beyond imaginable limits to fulfill it. Yet as liberated as they were from the paralyzing political passivity of diaspora Judaism, they were constricted by other contradictions in modern Jewish history. Their repudiation of rabbinic Judaism surely energized them for their task of state-building. But their vision of political Zionism, severed from Jewish sources and attached to universalist fantasies of Jewish normalization, was nearing a dead end of spiritual hollowness in modern Israel.

In this void, the religious faith and historical consciousness of the Jews of Judea and Samaria tapped a new reservoir of Zionist passion. Their synthesis of Zionism and Torah, Jewish land and Jewish law, pointedly reminded secular Jews (who indulgently absorbed every passing political and cultural fashion and called it Judaism) what they had abandoned. Oz might cherish the freedom "to decide what I will choose from this great [Jewish] inheritance, to decide what I will place in my living room and what I will relegate to the attic." (So, of course, did I.) Yet precisely that freedom explained the determination of the Jews of Hebron to reclaim their biblical patrimony.

More than twenty-five years after Judea and Samaria were restored to the Jewish people, Orthodox nationalists and their secular liberal critics still bitterly contested their competing claims to Jewish authenticity. Tribalists and universalists remained hopelessly divided by the fateful split between Jewish history and Western modernity. Modern Jews certainly are free to choose, but my allegiance was with those who remain loyal to the Land of Israel, not the land of Oz.

The Old City of Jerusalem, I learned from years of wandering, does not easily reveal its secrets to strangers. Its quarters—Jewish, Armenian, Christian, Moslem—are merely modern boundaries of convenience, the residue of British efforts to impose Western order in the Middle East. The maze of streets, winding through the *shuk* and bending around holy sites (both real and imaginary), entices visitors into distant time and foreign space.

Despite the teeming street life within the ancient city, its inhabitants are elusive, often concealing themselves behind metal doors, iron gates, shuttered windows, and stone walls. I discovered Ethiopians living on top of the Holy Sepulchre Church, Moors whose ancestors came as African slaves to serve their Moslem masters, Arabs whose dingy shops in the dankest alleys opened upon majestic gardens, and Armenians whose sprawling church property remains their lingering memorial to ancient national longings.

I even discovered Jews living in the Moslem Quarter. "We are not here to make anyone angry," Raya insisted with quiet firmness. But, she added, "We love Jerusalem." That hardly differentiated this intense woman, a mother in her thirties, from Jews through the ages, whose timeless longing for their holy city was recorded in Psalm 137 during the Babylonian exile. Nor, among modern Jews, is Raya's family history unique. Her mother left Poland for Palestine in 1932, serving in the Palmach during Israel's struggle for independence. Her father, who escaped from Hungary during World

War II, lived in Kfar Etzion, between Jerusalem and Hebron, until it fell to the Arabs in 1948.

Thirty years later, Raya and her husband Yossi, like earlier generations of Zionist *halutzim* in the *kibbutzim* sprinkled through the northern Galilee and southern Negev, located a place in Eretz Israel that needed Jews. Then they settled there. Their place was Jerusalem. They moved into Beit Maaravim, a building that for nearly a century had belonged to the Moroccan Jewish community. Their decision, Raya recalled with a shrug, was undramatic. They were, however, virtually the first Jewish family to live in the Old City, outside the Jewish Quarter, in fifty years.

"We were here alone and nobody came," Raya recounted, her expression tightening at the memory. Had we made a terrible mistake, she wondered? But Yossi reassured her: "It can not be that we did not do the right thing. Jerusalem must be rebuilt." Not long after their move, Yossi was called into the army for a month of reserve duty. "I stayed alone," Raya continued, the only Jewish woman living in the Moslem Quarter. Other students from the yeshiva where Yossi studied stopped by constantly to reassure her but, she remembered, "I felt so lonely." Several months later, another Jewish family moved nearby, followed by three more. "When you believe in your way," Raya smiled, "you must go on with it."

The way of Raya and Yossi, joined by more than forty other Jewish families, seems incomprehensible—if not outrageous—to Arabs, American Jews, and most Israelis. They are the vanguard of Ateret Cohanim (Crown of Priests), a yeshiva yearning to inspire a national and religious movement. Ateret Cohanim, in the words of its rabbi, "aspires to renew the Jewish presence in the heart of Jerusalem." Rabbi Shlomo Aviner, incongruously, is both a Sorbonne graduate with a degree in electrical engineering and a disciple of Rabbi Zvi Yehuda Kook, whose teachings inspired Gush Emunim. Israel, Rabbi Aviner has written, needs Jews "who are faithful to both the Torah and the nation." But when he refers to "a movement that believes in the hand of G-d . . . [who] will not disavow His commitment to His people," he is likely to make secular Israelis, dreaming of Volvos, VCRs, and vacations abroad, squirm with discomfort.

Why, I asked Mati, one of the movement pioneers, did you come to the Old City? *"Beshert"* (fate), he replied instantly. (Then, for a moment, his engaging smile froze and he inverted my question: "You are a Jew?" Yes. "Then why are you not here?") His parents lived for a time in kibbutz Sde Eliahu; now, he muses wryly, he lives in Beit Eliahu (known also as Galizia, after its original Polish Jewish residents). Mati shrugged aside his act of pioneering faith. *"Lisgor maagal,"* he said: "the circle is completed."

What is now the "Moslem" Quarter was, many centuries ago, the Jewish Quarter. Indeed, until the 1930s, the Old City remained a patchwork of ethnically and religiously mixed neighborhoods. According to a 1921 Jerusalem directory, 297 Jewish families (totaling 812 "souls") lived in the Damascus Gate area, as many Jews as inhabited the crowded Orthodox enclave of Mea Shearim. The directory also lists Rabbi Zerech Epstein's yeshiva on Hagai Street and a number of stores owned by Jews near Herod's Gate in the Moslem Quarter and adjacent to Muristan in the Christian Quarter. After the Arab riots of 1936–39, however, British Mandatory authorities pacified the Arabs by relocating Old City Jews to the ghetto that became known as the Jewish Quarter.

The theme of return, restoration, and renewal is fundamental to the sense of purpose among the Jews of Ateret Cohanim. Many of their properties inside Herod's Gate, along Hagai Street, or adjacent to the Temple Mount, once were owned by Jews and nestled within flourishing Jewish neighborhoods. I visited the Wittenberg house; like Galizia, it has been owned by Jews since the nineteenth century. Purchased from the Latin Catholic Church by Rabbi Moshe Wittenberg, it once housed twenty Jewish families, a library, and a *bet knesset.* Since the 1890s, the building has been held in trust "to sustain Jewish life in Jerusalem in perpetuity." Spanning Hagai Street, a hundred meters inside Damascus Gate, its handsome double tier of curved windows above an arched tunnel straddles the major north-south axis of the Old City.

Like other Jewish properties nearby, the Wittenberg house was abandoned during the Arab riots. Once graceful and elegant, it became home to Arab squatters, its interior courtyards drug-infested hovels in a tawdry neighborhood adjacent to the Austrian Hospice. Just a few years ago, however, it suddenly gained a different kind of notoriety, international in scope, when Ariel Sharon, the controversial housing minister of Israel, purchased an apartment in the building and declared it his primary residence. Sharon's characteristically bold gesture transformed the Wittenberg house. The constant presence of Israeli soldiers at the entrance, a perquisite of Cabinet ministers, secured the property, now the residence of two Arab and two Jewish families and the Ateret Cohanim security center.

Down Hagai Street, at the bend in the Via Dolorosa as it winds its way up to the Church of the Holy Sepulchre, is the Ateret Cohanim yeshiva, listed in the 1921 Jerusalem directory under Rabbi Epstein's name as the Torat Chaim yeshiva. The sign from the old yeshiva, founded by Grand Rabbi Isaac Winograd in 1886, still adorns the outer wall of the building. An Israeli flag flutters over the entrance. Inside, up the staircase, past the dingy apartment of a resident Arab family, is the flourishing yeshiva where nearly two hundred students study. The morning of my visit, an ordinary Monday, two dozen males, ranging in age from ten to seventy, were reading, reciting, debating—intensely engaged in traditional Talmudic *lernen*.

The Jews of Ateret Cohanim are unfazed by their hostile critics. Raya smiled as she recounted her decision, twelve years ago, "to be the crazy one." She spoke of a family gathering of the parents of the Ateret Cohanim community and a song that she composed for the occasion. Its theme was: "We did what you did. We follow your footsteps." Just as previous generations of Zionists persevered and prevailed against the insurmountable odds of Arab violence and Jewish apathy, so, Raya insists, will they. Danny, her neighbor, who was stabbed in the back when he took his one-year-old son into the Arab *shuk* to buy bananas, added sharply: "There is no boundary in Jerusalem for Jews."

Etty, Mati's wife, echoed the theme of generational continuity. She noted, proudly, that their parents (her mother came from a French Communist family and her father is an Israeli sabra) "changed the land." But every generation "wants to do, to build." After 1967, among her modern Orthodox friends, the dream was to rebuild Jerusalem. "There cannot be a ghetto in Jerusalem," Etty added, her soft voice firm and her dark eyes flashing as she rocked her young son. "We do not provoke; we are just people who live here, to build Jerusalem."

Secular Israelis (led for many years by Mayor Teddy Kollek of Jerusalem) have insisted that Arab hostility is a sufficient deterrent, at least for now, to a restored Jewish presence in the Moslem Quarter. Jews, after all, may have the "right" to live anywhere in Eretz Israel, but it is sheer folly to exercise it in such hostile surroundings. I recalled this criticism during two delightful days of family hiking, swimming, and kayaking in the northern Galilee. We stayed in a venerable Labor Zionist kibbutz, just down the road from biblical Dan and Banias. A few kilometers from the Lebanese border, it is enclosed by a barbed-wire fence; its security gate, constantly monitored, closes at twilight. I assumed that the guard, like Ateret Cohanim security guards in the Old City, had instant access to a walkie-talkie and a gun. No one suggested that it was inappropriate for Jews to live here.

The torch of Zionist passion had long since passed from secular Israelis, whose creative energies subsided by the end of the Ben-Gurion years, to religious Zionists, galvanized by the Six Day War. From Degania, the first kibbutz, to Rabbi Kook's Mercaz HaRav yeshiva, the cradle of Gush Emunim, Zionism had changed but Zionism endured. After 1967, the Torah, not Marxian socialism, became the source of Zionist inspiration. "We read the Hebrew Bible," Danny asserted, "and we know where we are going."

I visited Ateret Cohanim families just after the Israeli election of 1992, when the sighs of relief from American Jews over Yitzhak Rabin's victory were audible even in Jerusalem. Rabin's election meant that happy days were here again. No more allegations of disloyalty from American presidents. No more complaints about Israel's "Amen" corner in Congress. No more media-bashing of Israel for its refusal to capitulate to Arab violence and international pressure. Once Israeli and American policies dovetailed and the taint of American disloyalty was removed, Jewish liberals could hardly contain their joy.

Many American Jews (and Israelis) welcomed Rabin as the messiah of liberal Zionism. But his evident willingness to relinquish Judea and Samaria for a Palestinian state signified to me the spiritual exhaustion of secular Zionism. It had become a tired movement, finally battered into submission by the Palestinian *intifada*, Iraqi SCUDs, and its own weariness with the burden of Jewish history. Now, after decades of struggle, Israelis were prepared to capitulate to their enemies in the name of Zionist normalization.

I found it refreshing, instead, to be among Jews who did not apologize for their Jewish passion. God, it is often said, is on the side of the largest battalions. The Jews of Ateret Cohanim, like the Jews of Hebron, are not convinced. God, Etty believes, "is in this place." Perhaps she is right.

Abraham, the Bible tells us, heard the command, *Lech l'cha*: "Get thee out of thy country, and from thy kindred, and from thy father's house, to the land that I will show thee." And he obeyed. Uprooted, leaving his father, his family, and his people for an unknown destination, he had only his faith to sustain him. But it sufficed.

I imagine my grandfather Jacob, like countless other Eastern European Jews of his time, summoned by a voice of irresistible power to begin a hazardous journey to a strange land. Surely he did not leave Romania because he heard a divine command; more likely, he emigrated because he no longer heard God's voice. Probably the cry of privation, and the siren song of American opportunity, uprooted him. Jacob lived out his days in his adopted land; yet, like Abraham, he remained a stranger, a sojourner.

The children of immigrants may pay dearly for parental boldness. Consider Isaac, passively bound by the plans that others made for him. In the *Akedah*, he was suspended at the edge of death to enable Abraham to display his own unremitting faith in divine will. Rebekah, the woman he married, was chosen by his father's servant. Uneasy with change or challenge, Isaac spent much of his adult life, according to the biblical narrative, redigging his father's wells. In old age, with his vision (and insight) dimmed, he was deceived by his wife and son into diverting Esau's birthright to Jacob. Isaac was a survivor, not a creator; he was there, he endured.

So it was with my father, the immigrant's son. Deprived by Jacob's premature death of an opportunity to shape his own life, he tunneled his vision to provide for the family that depended on him. With unrelenting self-sacrifice he made the needs of others into his own. Like Isaac, he must have found it risky to assert his own wishes, or even to acknowledge that he had them. For second-generation American Jews like my father, the "real work" of their lives, Philip Roth has written, "was making themselves American."

Instructed by my father's example, I retreated behind the mask of Jewish self-denial. I could always find other Jews like me, for they were everywhere in my generation. As the very model of an enlightened non-Jewish Jew by the time I reached adulthood, I stood at the brink of Jewish oblivion.

But in the third generation, the biblical paradigm suggests, re-pressed generational tensions can erupt in a fierce attempt to define and secure the family legacy. Abraham responded and Isaac sub-mitted, but Jacob struggled. In the transforming experience of his life, he grappled in lonely solitude with "a man"—whether an an-gel, the divine spirit, or his own inner self is left purposely am-biguous by the text—to secure his own birthright. Finally granted his elusive blessing, he was renamed (reborn) Israel. His struggle forever identified him as the patriarch of the tribes that fused into the nation that still bears his name.

When the biblical Jacob became Israel, endowed with the new name that God gave to him, he assumed responsibility for preserv-ing and transmitting the distinctive heritage of his people. The children of Israel, Jacob's children, inherited the patriarchal legacy. In Israel, where my struggle with Jacob's legacy began, I finally encountered my grandfather Jacob, the Jacob within me. As Jacob and Israel converged for me, I was returned to my family, to the history of my people, and to our promised land.

When I began to compose our family history for my father's seventy-fifth birthday, nearly twenty years ago, I must have been desperate to hear Jacob's voice, his Jewish voice, before it became forever inaudible. I often wondered about Jacob's fateful decision to emigrate. He might have remained in Botosoni with his sisters, two of whom survived World War II and moved to Israel. What then—for him, for my father, for me, for my children? But a man in his early thirties, with a new wife and young baby, would sacrifice everything for American opportunity. It pulled him west to the

United States, not east to Palestine. His decision made the difference for all of us.

My father seemed slightly uncomfortable with my celebration of Jacob as our family patriarch. To become what America demanded of him, my father had all but relinquished his Jewish birthright. Yet I was trying to tell him, however obliquely, that despite his best efforts to erase our antecedents in the shtetl culture of Eastern Europe, I would no longer permit it. I had absorbed all his messages of accommodation and assimilation, while learning that Judaism was excess baggage to be left behind for American rewards. Now I needed to hear Jacob's voice. Then, finally, I might discover my own.

Romania had failed Jacob, so he fled. Yet we shared something in common, my grandfather and I, for we both lived in prolonged spiritual exile in the United States. Despite my intimate familiarity with a culture that he could barely have comprehended, it had ceased to belong to me at an early age. Yet I could not leave it behind; indeed, I became a chronicler of its past. When I finally felt the power of Zionist imperatives, I was too much a creature of the diaspora to choose yet another form of exile.

The painful moment of comprehension came one morning in Jerusalem, during my Jubilee sabbatical. I had been struggling at my desk for weeks to find the precise words to express some tangled Jewish issue whose meaning was not yet clear to me. As a scholar whose life was words, I felt trapped between languages and the cultures they expressed, the fluent English that had always ordered my thoughts as an American and the fractured Hebrew that had begun to orchestrate my feelings as a Jew. If I remained in Israel, I sensed apprehensively, English might become a foreign language. I might even lose my writer's voice, my only voice. Then I understood why I would return to the United States. Only in English, the Christian language that was mine but not mine, could I translate Jacob's voice into my own.

When my father died, as my son poignantly observed at the funeral, there no longer was anyone in our family who had known Jacob. A single death left us doubly diminished. In more than name, I sensed, I had become the family Jacob, whose task it was to secure the family birthright. I felt the power of the biblical command to the children of Israel: Remember. Remember the commandments. Remember Egyptian slavery. Remember Amalek. Remember Zion. And, as Moses implores in his majestic farewell poem:

> Remember the days of old
> Consider the years of many generations:
> Ask your father and he will recount it to you.

Now it was my turn to remember, and to recount. But it is so difficult for the Jews of modernity to remember. If Jacob remembered, he did not speak; if my father heard, he could not remember. Amnesia was our family legacy. After my father's death, as the calibrated stages of mourning receded, only memory endured as the link between us.

Each year since his death, during the several weeks that span his birthday, his *yahrzeit*, and the *Yizkor* memorial service of Yom Kippur, I draw close to my father through ritually structured memory. Walking along the cemetery road to his grave, I can almost evoke the world that framed my grandfather's childhood in Botosoni and my father's childhood in Pittsburgh. That world, like my father, is gone now, forever, irrevocably lost. But the cemetery road draws me close to him; it returns me to our family journey from Eastern Europe, connecting me to my Jewish past.

I know that once the shackles of ghetto life crumbled in the modern era, as Gershom Scholem has written, "the internal restraints of the Jews against Western culture were also relaxed." As the enticements of modernity dissolved Jewish memory, Jews were tantalized by the limitless opportunities of freedom to define themselves, and to define themselves as Jews. "In the final analysis," David Biale suggests, "all contemporary Jews . . . are Jews by choice." But Biale's pro-choice Judaism, in which "all the possibilities . . . [can] be taken as equally legitimate," denies the very notion of Jewish legitimacy. Judaism becomes a sponge, soggy with all that it absorbs from external sources. Any distinction between Judaism and everything else is all but obliterated.

Judaism, to be sure, has always been historically malleable. Yet it succeeded remarkably well, until relatively recently, in protecting its own boundaries. But pro-choice Jews, ever attentive to the latest gossip in the global village, are intensely uneasy with any Jewish self-identification that focuses upon Israel, Jewish law, religious observance, or even Jewish self-interest. They want nothing to do with a "holy nation" that "dwells alone." Anything that is anchored in discomforting notions of Jewish distinctiveness becomes stifling, xenophobic, arrogant. While all other peoples (especially, it seems, Palestinians) are entitled to pursue their own self-centered visions, only Jews are constrained.

But if we are all pro-choice Jews in the modern era, then Jewish distinctiveness surely is as valid a choice as any other, with far stronger Jewish historical credentials than most. I might be too American to relinquish the freedom of choice that modernity bestows. And if *aliya* measures commitment, as Israelis have every reason to insist, then I am not even a Zionist. But in Israel, enclosed in Jewish space and time, I learned to appreciate the prophet Jeremiah's admonition: "ask for the old paths, where the good way is." That may be enough.

Yet I wonder if my children will ask me to recount "the years of many generations," and whether they will remember what I can tell them. Will they be charmed by the breathless enthusiasm of American Jewish Pollyannas, exulting that Jews are finally and truly at home in the United States? Or will they learn how destructive of Judaism the comforts of their American home can become? I would like them to believe that their great-grandfather Jacob chose wisely in seeking refuge in the United States, but occasionally I am uncertain. Perhaps they, too, will find in their own community of committed Jews some possibilities for Jewish continuity.

Even if they do, however, that may only compound the irony of their lives as American Jews. For as David Vital has written, "the more conscious Diaspora Jews are of their special identity and ancestral roots and the more highly they value them, the more powerfully Israel saps at the foundations of their communities." If my children are ever to hear Jacob's voice for themselves, they may have to listen for it in Israel, where Jewish history and destiny seem finally to have converged.

Yet in Israel, too, the bonds of Jewish memory have frayed ominously thin. The relentless pressures of secular modernity erode Jewish life in the Jewish state, no less than in the diaspora. The Zionist dream of normalization contains its own hidden paradox: the more normal that Israel becomes, and the more avidly that Israelis embrace Western cultural and intellectual fashion, the more closely they resemble those nineteenth-century diaspora Jews who rushed to emulate the manners and mores of their Christian emancipators.

Two Israeli traumas, twenty years apart, framed the transformation that I had witnessed in Zionist consciousness. For Israelis, as for Jews everywhere, the outbreak of war on Yom Kippur, in October 1973, not only demonstrated an unrelenting Arab determination to eliminate the Jewish state, but a terrifying expression of Islamic *jihad*. To Jews, the point needed no elaboration; the date chosen by Arabs for attack, on the holiest day of the Jewish calendar, hardly was random. That Yom Kippur morning, as Harold Fisch wrote, "A metaphysical shudder . . . passed through the body of Israel."

Twenty years later, in September 1993, the world was riveted by the handshake in Washington between Yitzhak Rabin and Yasir Arafat. But I watched faces, not hands. Arafat exulted, for good reason: his PLO, wracked by internal conflict, verging on financial ruin, spurned by Arab states, and diminished in the media by newer claimants to superior victim status, had just been rescued from terminal collapse by the government of Israel. Rabin, however, was funereal, for his government suddenly existed for no purpose other than to divest the Jewish state of its biblical homeland, the geographical and historical cradle of Jewish civilization. Zionism, I realized sorrowfully, had all but lost its will to continue the struggle against its rival claimant for the Land of Israel. That was even more devastating than the terrible Yom Kippur, twenty years earlier, when the determination of Israelis to resist their enemies was unquestioned and undiminished. Now, however, their loftiest ambition seemed to be the conversion of their country into an appendage of Western consumer culture, a Middle Eastern version of the American dream, without any discernible Jewish content. With Zionism too burdensome to bear, the lure of Western normality—

McDonald's and Pizza Hut, cellular phones and microchips—was too enticing to resist.

I sensed, in the Land of Israel, a widening chasm between Zionism and Judaism. In our *minyan*, one *Shabbat* morning, an Israeli visitor presumptuously instructed us about our *galut* deficiencies. How could we fail to understand, this secular Zionist wondered, that God wanted Jews to be there, not here. Yet his coterie of Israeli friends, who came to a synagogue only to celebrate his son's bar mitzvah, certainly seemed oblivious to divine wishes. Barely able to distinguish a *siddur* from the *Chumash*, they had long since drifted into boredom and chatter. I lost their Hebrew words but the meaning was clear: you can take Jews out of *galut*; but even in Israel, it seems, you cannot take *galut* out of the Jews.

The Temple was destroyed, we are taught, by *sinat hinam*—groundless hatred between Jews. I detected such hatred within the Jewish state, emanating from Israelis whose secular Zionism sets peaceful normality above its highest joy. Perhaps the time will come when these secular fundamentalists can confront the darker side of their own Zionism. They passionately advocate peace with Arabs in *keffiyahs*, yet they are at war with Jews who wear *kippot* and *t'fillin*. They have forgotten, if they ever learned, that Zionism not only requires a Jewish state but a Jewish state of mind. For Zionism without Judaism means nothing less than the abandonment of Jewish covenantal history and memory. Israelis, too, might heed the Baal Shem Tov, founder of Hasidism, who warned: "Forgetfulness leads to exile, while remembrance is the secret of redemption."

The ancient polarity of Jerusalem and Babylon, and the creativity and endurance of Jewish communities in exile, suggest that bets on Jewish geography may always need to be hedged. Jeremiah, after all, praised the exiles in Babylon as "good figs," for their undiminished loyalty to God. The "bad figs," who remained behind in Jerusalem, were a "horror for evil." And Jeremiah's landscape for prophetic denunciation did not even include Tel Aviv. But the prophet understood that exile and home need not be fixed geographical locations.

The wheel of Jewish historical fortune has turned, too terribly and wonderously in my own life, for me to be certain that authentic

Jewish voices can be heard only in the Jewish state. If normalization is all there is to Zionism, then Israelis may yet confront the mournful reality that they, too, are in exile at home. Israel can hardly remain the land of Jewish destiny once Judaism atrophies in Zion.

I surround myself in my American home with antiquities dug from tombs in Hebron, Shechem, and Jerusalem; centuries-old maps of biblical Israel; family relics; and books that trace my scholarly itinerary from American history, through law, to American Jewish history and, finally, to Israel. There is also my assortment of antique scales (including a tiny jeweler's scale made three centuries ago by another Jew named Jacob who lived in Cologne, not far from the village of Auerbach). They help me to weigh and balance the conflicting claims that engage me.

I work at my desk under the scrutiny of my grandfather and my father, who draw closer to me the longer we are separated. I am, I know, both of them: the generational fusion of shtetl Orthodoxy and American assimilation. I am too much my father's son to be anything but an uncomfortable, occasional visitor to Jacob's world; but I am too much Jacob's namesake ever to concede the final word to my father.

There are other photographs nearby, triggering memories of what I never knew but cannot forget. One, from Romania, shows a horse-drawn hearse outside a Jewish cemetery on a bleak, snowy day. A hunched old man, the only visible mourner, shuffles toward the open gate. He might as well be the last Jew in Romania. The horse has turned its head back to watch, as though in silent witness to the death of Romanian Jewry.

Another picture, quite well known, is from Warsaw. Taken during the last days of the Ghetto, it preserves the look of haunted terror on the face of a young boy exiting from a bunker with his hands raised in abject surrender to Nazi storm troops. He is carefully dressed—cap, coat, shorts, knee-socks, school bag—as though his mother had prepared him for a trip, his final journey as it turned out, surely to Treblinka. We were the same age when the photograph was taken. He reminds me of who, but for Jacob, I might have been. In his face I see my own reflection as a young boy, when Jacob came to visit. I know that if Jacob had not left Romania, this Jewish boy and I might have died together. Perhaps, it sometimes tortures me, he died in my place.

Finally, there is a photograph of the Western Wall, taken during the years of the British Mandate. Some Jews lean against it in prayer, others huddle nearby. I recognize the cracks and crevices in those courses of ancient stones, for I, too, have touched them. Although the faces are hidden, I know that I have seen them here, in Jerusalem by the Wall, many times. For nearly two thousand years, Jews have come here to come home, to remember. Here, when I heard Jacob's voice at last, I finally knew why. If I do not remember, my children will surely forget.

EPILOGUE

REBECCA, MY YOUNGEST DAUGHTER, THEN SEVEN years old, was standing with me at the kitchen sink, vigorously peeling potatoes for Susan's fabled Chanukah *latkes*. Shira, befitting her name, was singing nearby as she collated our tapes of Chanukah songs. Jeff and Pammy were expected soon. Candle-lighting was moments away. Amid the bustle, I began to narrate the story of the Maccabees to Rebecca.

I had barely reached Antiochus when I realized that I had a problem: the Chanukah story was *two* stories, and I wanted my daughter to understand both the popular version and the more subversive subtext. The rabbis, wishing to emphasize the divine miracle of a tiny cruse of oil that burned for eight nights, preferred to suppress the act of political rebellion that initiated it. But I did not feel comfortable merely reiterating the rabbinical version, however compelling an affirmation of divine power it conveyed.

Nor was that all. Introducing Rebecca to Mattathias, I recalled how disconcerted I had been, some years earlier, upon reading the historical narrative in *The First Book of Maccabees*. Mattathias, as Jews still recall with pride, boldly proclaimed to the officers of Antiochus: "I and my sons and my brethren walk in the covenant of our fathers. Heaven forbid that we should forsake the Law." But a Jew, eager to comply with Gentile authority, came forward to obey the royal decree for idolatrous worship. Mattathias's "zeal was kindled" by this apostasy. He killed the Jew first and then the royal officer, crying out, "Let everyone that is zealous for the Law . . . follow me!"

What does it mean (and not only to seven-year-olds) that the first target of Maccabean wrath was a Hellenized, assimilated Jew? If the Chanukah story bears perennial retelling, are not we Jews of modernity obligated to confront that sobering fact? Now as then, the adaptation of Judaism to Western civilization excites many Jews. Hellenism, so urban, urbane, and international, certainly was enticing two thousand years ago. Not much has changed. Greek theatre, to be sure, has yielded to VCRs. The *gymnasium* has been replaced by Disney World. The glories of ancient art and architecture have become the technological miracle of pentium chips. But the problem of Jewish assimilation endures, in Israel no less than in the diaspora.

In those days, the Maccabee narrative recounts, "there came forth out of Israel lawless men, and persuaded many, saying, 'Let us go and make a covenant with the nations that are round about us; for since we separated ourselves from them many evils have come upon us.' " In these days, during this very Chanukah, Israel's covenant with the PLO was completed. And in the hill towns of Judea, embattled Jews, zealous for the Law, struggle to repel the Hellenized enemy that still lurks within the Jewish people.

Chanukah is ever more enthusiastically celebrated in the American diaspora. Bloated and sweetened to compete with Christmas and to make Jews feel comfortable as an American minority, the Chanukah message of Jewish zeal in the face of assimilation is too threatening to disclose. Which Chanukah story should I tell my children? The story of a divine miracle, or the story of a desperate political rebellion to cleanse the assimilated soul of Judaism? Do we follow the Maccabees of our time or are we already too ravaged by modern Hellenism to recognize them?

Jewish tradition is too complex and nuanced to provide unambiguous guidance, even for the preservation of Judaism itself. If there was Mattathias, the bold rebel, there was also Joseph, the unabashed court Jew in Pharaoh's Egypt. Not to mention Esther, whose beauty and guile persuaded King Ahasuerus to save the Jews from Haman (so that they might, in turn, slaughter their Persian enemies). Even after the rabbis controlled the writing of Jewish history, they disagreed about strategies for Jewish survival. According to legend, Rabbi Yohanan ben Zakkai, who opposed the Zealots during their first-century rebellion against Rome, arranged to have himself smuggled from Jerusalem disguised as a corpse to secure Roman permission for a rabbinical academy at Yavneh for the study of Torah. Just a century later, however, Rabbi Akiva, who avidly supported the Bar Kokhba revolt, became an enduring and revered symbol of Jewish martyrdom.

Jewish paths diverge according to historical chance and circumstance. Some lead back to Zion; others meander through the diaspora. But a living people still needs the texts and traditions, the sacred time and holy space, the freedom and structure, that have preserved Israel and defined Judaism during five millennia. It is an "extraordinary privilege," Harold Fisch has written, for a Jew to participate in the "historical adventure" of the Jewish people—whether, I must add, in Zion or *galut*. An attentive modern Jew still can hear vibrant echoes of Jacob's ancient voice. I know that the story I tell my children, including the story of my own life, must begin and end here.

ACKNOWLEDGMENTS MY EXCURSION INTO AUTO-
biographical solitude was
immeasurably enriched by the loving kindness of friends and
family.

Michael Rosenthal, Stanley Fisher, Michael Meltsner, and Haggai
Hurvitz have been intimate friends for so long that I can hardly
imagine my life, or its retelling, without them. Their caring responses to an early manuscript draft deepened our shared memories while reaffirming the indissoluble bonds between us. Trudy
Fagen and Melinda Strauss were sensitive to the story that I was
trying to write even as they coaxed me, in their own distinctive
ways, to tell it better. Bill Novak, uncommonly wise in the arcane
intricacies of writing and publishing, offered encouragement and
consolation at the important moments.

Les Fagen, Irle Goldman, David Strauss, Allen Spivak, and Len
Lyons were attentive secret sharers. Jerome Rogoff helped me to
untangle some complicated knots, both autobiographical and sty-
listic. Edward Alexander was immensely helpful when it mattered
most. Jonathan Sarna, Mel Urofsky, and Steve Whitfield offered
valuable editorial counsel. James D. Simmons and Carol A. Burns
of Southern Illinois University Press responded graciously and generously to my assorted requests. Tracey Moore was a demanding
copy editor whose skill I appreciate.

My family nourished and sustained the life that I was simultaneously living, reliving, and telling. This book, in so many ways,
is for my children, Rebecca, Shira, Pamela, and Jeffrey, with grati-
tude for all the wonders of fathering they have bestowed. My wife,

Susan, may have been a reluctant participant in some of my more idiosyncratic Jewish forays, but for my life journey, I cannot imagine a companion more loving or loved.

September 1995
Elul 5755

JEROLD S. AUERBACH was born in Philadelphia and grew up in New York City. He attended the Horace Mann School, graduated from Oberlin College, and received his doctorate in history from Columbia University. He is the author of *Labor and Liberty* (1966), *Unequal Justice* (1976, a *New York Times* Noteworthy Book), *Justice Without Law?* (1983), and *Rabbis and Lawyers* (1990). His essays have appeared in *Commentary, Harper's,* the *New York Times,* the *New Republic,* the *Jerusalem Post,* and numerous Jewish periodicals. He has been a Guggenheim fellow, a Fulbright lecturer at Tel Aviv University, and a visiting scholar at Harvard Law School. He is a professor of history at Wellesley College, where he teaches courses in modern American history, American Jewish history, and the history of Israel.